INTRODUCTION TO DEFENDER'S PLAY

by Edwin B. Kantar

♠   ♡   ◇   ♣

WILSHIRE BOOK COMPANY
9731 VARIEL AVENUE
CHATSWORTH, CALIFORNIA 91311

Introduction to Defender's Play
by Edwin B. Kantar

© 1968 by Prentice-Hall, Inc.

Copyright under International and Pan American
Copyright Conventions

Library of Congress Catalog Card Number: 68-13004

Printed in the United States of America

T

Prentice-Hall International, Inc., *London*
Prentice-Hall of Australia, Pty. Ltd., *Sydney*
Prentice-Hall of Canada, Ltd., *Toronto*
Prentice-Hall of India Private Ltd., *New Delhi*
Prentice-Hall of Japan, Inc., *Tokyo*

ISBN 0-87980-322-3

Foreword

Contract Bridge is a game with many facets. In order to become an adept player, you must learn how to bid the hand, how to play the hand, how to compete in bidding, and how to offer a good defense.

Most books on Contract Bridge are written for the novice or inexperienced player. Many attempts to cover all parts in a single volume often result in only skimming the surface.

The Series concept developed by Prentice-Hall is especially good for teaching one how to play Contract Bridge—this book is one of four volumes in the Introductory Series. Although they are intended for beginners, each book contains great value for the intermediate as well as the near-expert player.

The author, Edwin B. Kantar, is one of America's leading young bridge experts and teachers. He was the coach of the 1967 North American Team that fared so favorably in the World Championships.

Edwin Kantar has contributed a regular column to the *American Contract Bridge League Bulletin* and has written over fifty articles for *The Bridge World* magazine. He is regarded as one of the outstanding world bridge experts on the play of the hand by declarer and defender.

ALVIN LANDY

Contents

Part I
DEFENSE VS. NOTRUMP

♠ ♡ ◇ ♣

♠ ♡ ◇ ♣

There is no question that defense is the most difficult aspect of playing bridge. Many players become adequate bidders by simply memorizing the point count for various bids; others find that playing a dummy becomes easy with practice. But, defense is a matter of *logic* and thus separates the men from the boys.

If you are a good defender it is almost impossible to be a losing player. At least half of your opponents' contracts can be defeated with a good defense, but the sad truth is that about eighty percent of them are fulfilled. Why?

Because most players have not been well-drilled in the fundamentals of defensive play: know the suit and the card in that suit to lead that will give partner the maximum amount of information; know when to signal; know when to play an attacking defense (taking your tricks as quickly as possible) as opposed to a passive defense (sitting back and waiting for your tricks); decide what the declarer is trying to do based on his manner of play. This is the blocking and tackling of bridge. You cannot be a good bridge player unless you can do these things with reasonable skill.

Because there is a considerable difference between defense against *notrump* contracts and defense against *suit* contracts, this book is divided into two parts. *Notrump* will be discussed first.

♠ ♡ ◇ ♣

1

The Opening Lead

♠ ♡ ◊ ♣

In order to be a good defender you must have some objectives in mind. What are they?

Go back and ask yourself how you play a hand as declarer. You try to establish your tricks before the defense can establish theirs. You are fortunate in that you can see the dummy and can usually tell which suit to establish. But even so you are almost always involved in a race.

The defenders, on the other hand, cannot see each other's cards and often will waste time trying to establish the wrong suit. However, the defenders have one great advantage that overshadows all else—they have the opening lead!

In other words, in the great "establishing" race the defenders always get off to a head start; and if you consistently make the proper opening lead, you will go down in history as one of the world's greatest players, even though your bidding and defense may be just average!

Why is it so hard to make the proper opening lead? Opening leads are based on the bidding and your hand. Sometimes the bidding makes it clear which suit to lead, other times you will have a clear-cut lead in your own hand, but much of the time you will be forced to make an intelligent guess because the bidding will not have given much away. Consider these two bidding sequences by your opponents:

SOUTH	WEST (you)	NORTH	EAST
1 NT	Pass	3 NT	Pass
Pass	Pass		

as opposed to:

SOUTH	WEST (you)	NORTH	EAST
1 ♣	Pass	1 ◊	Pass
3 ♣	Pass	3 ◊	Pass
3 NT	Pass	Pass	Pass

In both cases as West you have to make the opening lead. In the first case your partner hasn't bid and the opponents have given away very little information. They may have a weakness somewhere but you cannot be sure where.

Now take the second case. South has excellent clubs and North good diamonds. As West, you can eliminate a club or a diamond as a possible opening lead because you don't want to waste your lead establishing the opponents' suits. You would select either a heart or a spade lead depending upon your hand.

The important point is: listen to the bidding. *You must listen to the bidding; you can't even begin to defend unless you do.*

As a general rule, the declarer will establish his longest suit first, and the defense tries to do the same—the most logical way being to lead it. *That is why, with nothing else to go by, the opening leader leads from length.* Notice the key words, "with nothing else to go by." However, many times you are provided with plenty of information: your partner may have bid, or the opponents may have bid your longest suit. In such cases you would probably select another lead.

Assume, for the sake of argument, that after listening to the bidding you have decided to lead your longest suit, as this is by far the most common lead against notrump. Which card do you lead? Now look at a hand.

Sitting West, you hold:

♠ A 8 6 5 3   ♡ J 7 4 2   ◊ Q 3   ♣ 8 2

The bidding has proceeded: 1 NT on your right and 3 NT on your left. It is your lead. Now, if you could peek into your partner's hand and see that he had only one spade and five hearts you would lead a heart because that is your *combined* longest suit. Unfortunately, the rules do not permit this, so you must assume, because you have more spades, that spades is the longest combined suit. So you are going to lead a spade, but which spade?

Normally, when leading a suit that has four or more cards you lead your *fourth highest card*. Fourth highest means starting at the top and counting down four places. In this case your fourth highest spade would be the five. Don't make the mistake of starting at the bottom and counting up. *Start at the top and count down.*

That's simple enough, isn't it? What's the catch. The first catch is that your suit may have a three-card sequence, which simply means three equal cards at the head of the suit. For example, Q J 10 4 2 would be an example of a three-card sequence.

Whenever you hold a three-card sequence or longer at the head of your suit you always lead the *top of the sequence*. The sequence rule takes precedence over the fourth highest rule.

If the third card (the lowest card) in the three-card sequence is missing by one spot (Q J 9 2), it is still considered a sequence and the queen is led. However, if the third card drops off by more than one spot (Q J 8 2), you revert to the fourth best rule and lead the deuce.

Simply, the rule for leading from a suit of four or more cards is this: lead fourth highest unless the suit contains a sequence; if it does, lead the top of the sequence instead.

Which card would you lead from each of these combinations?

(a) K J 7 6 5	(d) K Q J 10 2	(g) J 10 7 6 4
(b) A 8 7 2	(e) K Q 10 8 5	(h) Q J 8 7 3 2
(c) K Q J 2	(f) K Q 8 4 3 2	(i) J 10 8 5 3

Solutions

(a)	The six	Fourth highest
(b)	The deuce	Fourth highest
(c)	The king	Top of a sequence

(d)	The king	Top of a sequence
(e)	The king	Top of a sequence (Third card in sequence missing by only one spot.)
(f)	The four	Fourth highest (You must have a three-card sequence before you can lead an honor card.)
(g)	The six	Fourth highest
(h)	The seven	Fourth highest
(i)	The jack	Top of a sequence

Sometimes you will have a choice of suits to lead. For example, sitting West you hold:

♠ Q 7 6 3   ♡ J 10 9 2   ◊ A 3   ♣ 5 4 2

Once again the bidding goes 1 NT on your right, 2 NT on your left, and everyone passes. It's your lead and you have two four-card suits. Which one should you lead? You should lead a heart—the jack, to be more specific. When holding two long suits, one of which contains a sequence, *you should lead the suit with the sequence.*

As a matter of fact, sequences are such fine leads that if you had the two of spades rather than the two of clubs you would still lead the jack of hearts, even though you had five spades and only four hearts.

Another possibility on opening lead is that your opponents may have bid your longest suit. Let's say you hold this hand:

♠ K 7 6 4 2   ♡ Q 10 4 2   ◊ J 10 7   ♣ 2

Again, you are West and your right-hand opponent bids 1 ♠, your left-hand opponent 2 ♣, 2 NT on your right, and 3 NT on your left. Your partner has been as silent as a mouse and it's your lead.

Had the opponents simply bid notrump without mentioning any suits, you would lead the four of spades. But spades have been bid, and it is usually a bad idea to lead suits the opponents have been bidding unless you have a sequence. So, we rule out a spade lead and lead our next-longest suit, hearts. The proper lead *on the bidding* would be the deuce of hearts.

Now let's keep the same hand but assume that our left-hand opponent bids 2 ♡ instead of 2 ♣. Once again, you are leading against notrump, only this time your opponents have bid both of your long suits! When you do not have a sequence in either of the bid suits, you normally select a lead from a three-card suit. In this case you would lead the jack of diamonds. But why the jack when you don't have a sequence?

When leading from a *three*-card suit, you must keep a few important points in mind. The most important is that the ten, jack, queen, king, and ace are considered honor cards. If you hold two touching honors and exactly three cards in the suit you must lead the higher honor. (The one exception to this is that from A K x you lead the king.)

Let's take a look at all the holdings that have *three* cards with two touching honors: A K x, K Q x, Q J x, J 10 x, 10 9 x. (Even though the nine is not considered an honor it is included in the list.) Remember that these are three-card holdings. If you have four or more cards in the suit you should lead fourth highest or top of a sequence, depending upon the size of the third card under the touching honors.

If you have three cards in the suit to be led headed by either one honor or by two non-touching honors, you must lead your *lowest* card. For example, if you were to lead from Q 10 4, you would lead the four. You have two *non-touching* honors, and from this type of holding you lead low.

Also, if you had A x x, K x x, Q x x, J x x, or 10 x x, you would lead your smallest card.

Finally, if you have three spot-cards, such as 8 4 2 or 9 7 5 or 6 5 3, lead the top card. This is called "top of nothing." Leads may be easier to remember if you repeat "top of nothing," "low from an honor," "top of a sequence," and "fourth highest" a few times.

The easiest of all rules to remember when making an initial lead covers which card to lead with a doubleton. With a doubleton, *always* lead the higher card first. Very often partner will

have thrown in a bid and you will be leading his suit. When you
have precisely two cards in that suit, lead the higher card.

The time has come to do a little reviewing. Which card
would you lead from each of the following holdings?

(a) J 9 7 5 3	(g) K Q 3 2	(m) K J 8 6 4 3
(b) J 7 5	(h) K 10 4	(n) Q 3
(c) 5 3	(i) A K 3	(o) 9 6 2
(d) Q J 9 7 3	(j) A K 7 5 2	(p) Q 7 4 2
(e) A 2	(k) 10 9 3 2	(q) 10 6 3
(f) K Q 3	(l) 10 9 4	(r) 4 3 2
		(s) K J 9 3 2

Solutions

(a)	The five	Fourth best
(b)	The five	Low from an honor
(c)	The five	Top of a doubleton
(d)	The queen	Top of a sequence
(e)	The ace	Top of a doubleton
(f)	The king	Top of two touching honors, when holding exactly three cards.
*(g)	The two	Fourth best, when holding two touching honors and more than three cards.
(h)	The four	Low from two honors when they are not touching in a three-card suit.
(i)	The king	This is the exception. When you hold exactly three cards, the king rather than the ace is led. (The lead of the ace *in an unbid suit* has a special meaning at no-trump, which we will come to shortly.)
*(j)	The five	Fourth best
(k)	The two	Fourth best
(l)	The ten	10 9 x is considered the same as two touching honors even though the nine is not an honor.

* But against a suit contract lead the king.

(m)	The six	Fourth best
(n)	The queen	Top of a doubleton
(o)	The nine	Top of nothing
(p)	The two	Fourth best
(q)	The three	Low from an honor (Remember that the ten is considered an honor.)
(r)	The four	Top of nothing
(s)	The three	Fourth best

These rules apply to the opening lead only! Common sense dictates your play *after* you see the dummy. For example, if dummy contains a singleton ace and you have K Q 10 6 in that suit, you should lead the six and not the king.

The reasons behind these opening leads are quite logical. Keep in mind that when you lead against notrump you will usually be leading a suit that has four or more cards. Your partner is aware of this and knows that you are leading from your long suit. Therefore, when you lead a low card from a holding such as K J 9 4 3, your partner will protect your holding by playing his highest card:

DUMMY

♠ 7 6

WEST (you)   EAST (partner)

♠ K J 9 4 3   ♠ Q 8 5

SOUTH

♠ A 10 2

Assume that you are defending a notrump contract and you lead the four of spades. Dummy plays low and your partner must play his queen. This protects your holding. If your partner refuses to play his queen and plays the eight instead, declarer makes two tricks rather than the one to which he is entitled.

You may wonder why you as West are leading fourth best from such a holding as:

DUMMY

♠ 9 8 6

WEST   EAST

♠ A K 7 5 3   ♠ 4 2

SOUTH

♠ Q J 10

If you were to lead the king, the ace, and then a third spade, South would win the trick. You would be left with two good spades, but your partner would not have a spade; if he then gained the lead he would not be able to return your suit.

If you first lead the five of spades, the declarer wins the trick; however, if your partner regains the lead he can return your suit and you can take your ace, your king, and your two little ones.

You must remember that at notrump you cannot lose an ace—since they cannot be trumped, you don't have to take all of your aces and kings immediately. You will recall that when you are playing a hand at notrump you seldom have enough sure tricks to make your contract; generally, you must establish and make good your lower honors as well as your lower cards. *The same applies to the defense.* They, too, must establish their lower cards if they wish to defeat most contracts, and the best way to do that is to lead fourth best from their longest suit.

We now have a few more combinations that we have not discussed and which simply must be memorized. These holdings include sequences in the middle of the suit, called "interior sequences"—holdings such as K J 10 9 3, A J 10 8 3, or simply K J 10 5 4 or A J 10 6. With any K J 10 or A J 10 holding the jack is led.

This naturally results in a little confusion, because the jack is also led from J 10 9 or J 10 8 combinations. The only thing that can be said is that when partner leads the jack you must be aware that he can conceivably have A J 10 or K J 10.

Similar holdings are A 10 9, K 10 9, and Q 10 9 with or without extended length. From these three holdings the ten is led. In other words, if you were to lead from K 10 9 6 3 you would lead the ten in preference to the six. Incidentally, these do not always work. Sometimes it turns out better to lead fourth highest from these holdings, especially if one of the opponents has bid the suit and you decide to lead it anyway. Nevertheless, most of the time a ten lead works out best.

If you have an inside sequence (interior sequence) beginning with a nine or less, *you still lead fourth best.* (From A 9 8 7 2, K 9 8 7 3, Q 9 8 7, or J 9 8 7 lead the seven.) In order to lead from the top of an interior sequence there must be at least one honor card in the sequence.

Finally, we come to the lead of the ace in an unbid suit. The lead of the ace against notrump asks partner to drop any high honor he may have in the suit!

Therefore the lead of the ace shows one of these holdings (with, perhaps, additional length):

AKJxxx   AKJ10   AKQ10   AQJ10

In other words, when you have all the honors but one in your suit and you want your partner to unblock and throw his honor, you lead the ace—obviously an unusual lead against notrump.

DUMMY

♠ 7 5 3

WEST   EAST

♠ A K J 10   ♠ Q 4

SOUTH

♠ 9 8 6 2

West leads the ace against notrump and East throws the queen as requested. If East does not throw the queen, West must assume that South has it, and he may make a mistake in the subsequent play.

Now that you know which card to lead from a good many

holdings and you realize how important it is to listen to the bidding, you are going to have a chance to test your new-found ability.

In each of the following problems you are to decide which card you would lead. You will always be West.

(a)   You hold:

♠ K J 7 5   ♡ Q J 9 6   ◊ 7 6   ♣ J 10 4

The bidding has proceeded:

SOUTH	WEST	NORTH	EAST
1 NT	Pass	3 NT	Pass
Pass	Pass		

(b)   You hold the same hand but this time the bidding has proceeded:

SOUTH	WEST	NORTH	EAST
1 ♠	Pass	2 ♡	Pass
2 NT	Pass	3 NT	Pass
Pass	Pass		

(c)   With the same hand again, the bidding has proceeded:

SOUTH	WEST	NORTH	EAST
1 ♠	Pass	2 ♣	2 ◊
2 NT	Pass	3 NT	Pass
Pass	Pass		

For each of the following five different hands to lead from, assume that in each case the bidding has gone:

SOUTH	WEST	NORTH	EAST
1 NT	Pass	3 NT	Pass
Pass	Pass		

(1)	♠ A K J 10	♡ 9 7 5 3 2	◊ 4 2	♣ 8 7
(2)	♠ Q J 10 6	♡ K 8 6 5 3	◊ 5 2	♣ J 7
(3)	♠ 8 6 3	♡ Q 8 4 2	◊ K 5	♣ Q 10 4 2
(4)	♠ J 8 6	♡ K 10 9 3 2	◊ J 7 6	♣ K 6
(5)	♠ 7	♡ J 9 8 7 6	◊ A 10 7 6	♣ Q 3 2

Solutions

(a)	The queen of hearts	The sequence lead is preferred over the non-sequence lead in spades.
(b)	The jack of clubs	Both of your suits have been bid, and unless you have a perfect sequence (Q J 10) you normally do not lead a suit that an opponent has bid at his first opportunity. Dummy will almost always have five hearts and you will be wasting your time leading a heart.
(c)	The seven of diamonds	This time your partner has told you what to lead.
(1)	The ace of spades	This asks your partner to unblock the queen if he has it.
(2)	The queen of spades	A sequence lead in a four-card suit takes precedence over a broken five-card holding.
(3)	The two of clubs	When both suits look about the same, lead the stronger of the two.
(4)	The ten of hearts	The ten is led from holdings which include A 10 9, K 10 9, or Q 10 9.
(5)	The seven of hearts	Do not be misled by the sequence in hearts. To justify a lead from the top of an interior sequence, the sequence

must be headed by the queen, jack or ten. A lead of the nine would guarantee no higher honor.

KEY POINTERS

(1)   In order to select the proper opening lead you must listen to the bidding.

(2)   With no clues in the bidding the opening leader normally leads his longest suit.

(3)   Sequence leads are better than fourth-best leads and take precedence over them. A four-card suit headed by a sequence is usually a better lead than a longer suit without a sequence.

(4)   Avoid leading suits that the opponents have bid unless you have three-card or longer sequences in those suits.

(5)   Aces, kings, queens, jacks, and tens are considered honor cards. The more honor cards you have in a particular suit the more apt you are to lead the suit. A lead from K 10 4 2 is preferable to a lead from K 8 6 2.

(6)   If partner has bid, especially if he has overcalled, you tend to lead his suit. The only exception is if you happen to have a very strong opening lead of your own (K Q J x x, for instance, with an outside entry).

(7)   When leading from length you lead either fourth highest or top of a sequence, unless you happen to have one of these holdings:

A J 10 or K J 10, in which case you lead the jack.

A 10 9, K 10 9, Q 10 9, A Q 10 9, or A K 10 9, in which case you lead the ten.

A K Q J, A K Q 10, A K J 10, A Q J 10, in which case you lead the ace.

(8)   When leading from a three-card holding headed by one honor (A x x, K x x, Q x x, J x x, 10 x x) you lead your lowest card.

When leading from a three-card holding headed by no honors 9̲ x x, 8̲ x x, 7̲ x x, etc. you lead your top card.

(9)   When leading from a three-card holding that has two honor cards, lead the top honor if they are touching and the lowest card if they are not. (An exception is A K̲ x.):

K̲ Q x, Q̲ J x, J̲ 10 x, 1̲0̲ 9 x, A J x̲, K J x̲, K 10 x̲, Q 10 x̲

(10)   When leading from any two-card holding, lead the top card.

(11)   The rules for leads apply to both the opening lead and any time the suit is being initiated later in the play—unless common sense dictates otherwise.

(12)   As a general rule, honor leads show sequences, high middle cards tend to be top of nothing, and low cards tend to be fourth best. The lead of the nine always denotes the highest card in that suit.

(13)   Always keep your objective in mind. You are trying to set up your suit or your partner's suit before declarer can set up his suit or suits. You have a head start because the defense makes the opening lead. Don't waste your opportunity.

2

Third-Hand Play to the First Trick

♠ ♡ ◇ ♣

As important as it is to select both the proper suit and the proper card in that suit for your opening lead against notrump, so is it for your partner to be able to "read your lead" and play properly to the first trick.

Generally, you will be leading either a low card (fourth best) or an honor card (top of a sequence) against notrump unless you happen to be leading your partner's suit, in which case you may be short suited.

The card that you lead, as well as the cards in the dummy, the cards in your partner's hand, and the bidding, all go into determining your partner's play to the first trick!

In the first chapter you were always West, making the opening lead. You are about to be switched over to the East side of the table, where you must start "reading" at your partner's lead. Let's start out by assuming your partner is leading a small card —for example, the deuce.

THIRD-HAND PLAY WITH TWO OR THREE SMALL CARDS IN DUMMY

DUMMY

♠ 7 6 3

WEST   EAST

♠ 2   ♠ K J 5

SOUTH

♠ ?

We are going to assume, for the sake of argument, that the bidding has been non-committal (1 NT by South, pass by West, 3 NT by North) and that your partner, West, has led the two of spades. After dummy plays the three, which one should you play sitting in the East position, and why?

Before answering, look at the entire diagram:

DUMMY

♠ 7 6 3

WEST   EAST

♠ A 10 8 2   ♠ K J 5

SOUTH

♠ Q 9 4

I hope you can see that if you play the king and then return the jack, South will be unable to take a single trick in the suit; but if you play the jack, South will win the queen—an undeserved trick.

What can we conclude from this diagram? We can say that when partner leads a low card and dummy has no honor cards (jack or higher) third hand must play its *highest* card unless it has two or three *equal* high cards. In that case third hand plays its lowest equal.

This simply means that if East had K Q 5 instead of K J 5 East would play the queen rather than the king. And if East happened to have K Q J 5 the jack would be the proper play.

The reason for third hand playing its highest card when partner leads low is to protect partner's holding in the suit and to prevent declarer from taking a cheap trick.

Now that you know the rule for third-hand play when partner leads low and there are no honor cards in the dummy, it's time to do a little practicing. Assuming that your partner has led the two of spades against a notrump contract and you have the following holdings, which card would you play?

DUMMY

♠ 7 6 3

WEST   EAST

♠ 2   (a) ♠ Q 10 9
               (b) ♠ A K 4
               (c) ♠ Q J 10 5
               (d) ♠ Q J
               (e) ♠ J 9 8 5

SOUTH

?

Solutions

(a) The queen   Third hand high when not holding equal high cards
(b) The king   Lower of two touching equals
(c) The ten   Lowest of three touching equals
(d) The jack   Lower of two touching equals
(e) The jack   Third hand high when not holding equal high cards

The moment has come to take stock of what is going on. It may seem confusing that when you have Q J 10 and *you* led the suit originally you lead the queen but when your *partner* leads the suit you play the ten. There are some very good reasons for this as you will soon realize.

In order to see how far you have progressed, assume that you are once again in the West position for a moment:

DUMMY

♠ 7 6 3

WEST   EAST

♠ Q 10 5 2   ♠ A

SOUTH

?

You lead the two of spades against a notrump contract by South, your partner takes the first trick with the ace, and South plays the four. Question: Who has the king?

With a little thought you should realize from your partner's play of the ace that South must have the king. If your partner had held both the ace and the king he would have played the king.

Try this one:

NORTH

♠ 7 6 3

WEST   EAST

♠ Q 9 8 4 2   ♠ J

DUMMY

♠ A

Again, you are West, and this time you lead the four of spades against South's notrump contract. East produces the jack, and South takes the trick with the ace. Who has the king and who has the ten?

The way to solve these is to ask yourself how your partner would have played if he had had these various cards.

If your partner had had the king and the jack, he would have played the king, not the jack. Remember that the rule is third hand high unless you hold *equal* high cards. The king and the jack are not equal, so East surely would have played the king if he had held it. Therefore, South is trying to mislead us by taking the first trick with the ace, but we know he has the king also.

But wait! Where's the ten? South must have it as well. If East had owned the jack and the ten he would have played the ten the first time. Therefore, South has both the king and the ten.

Are you beginning to see why it is so important for third hand to play the proper card to the first trick? *It informs the opening leader where the missing honors are.*

However, third hand's responsibility does not end with the

first trick. Very often he will wish to return the suit, and it is important that he know which card to return. Look at this a moment:

DUMMY

♠ 7 6

WEST   EAST

♠ A 9 8 5 2   ♠ K Q 4

SOUTH

♠ J 10 3

Occasionally your opponents will wind up in notrump without a stopper in one suit. It is inevitable. However, often that suit is not even led and declarer romps home easily.

Once in a while declarer gets caught and the proper suit is led, but even then the defense must know how to handle its riches.

In the hand above, West leads the five and East wins the trick with the *queen*. East now holds two cards, the king and four. *When you are left with exactly two cards in partner's suit you should return the higher of the two.* East must return the king, which takes the trick, and he then plays the four. West will win the third round of the suit with the ace, and both West's nine and eight will be good.

Notice what happens if East gets cold feet. If he returns the four at trick two, West wins the trick with his ace and then leads a third round to East's king. East has no more spades, and West is unable to cash his two remaining good spades.

There is nothing quite so aggravating in bridge as to have some good tricks only to find that when your partner gets the lead he has no more cards in your suit to lead to you.

What East is actually doing when he returns the king is unblocking his spades for West. Another way to look at this is to pretend that you are West playing the hand at notrump and you wish to take your good spades.

You will remember that when taking good tricks you should play the high card or cards from the short side first. West would play the king and queen of spades and then a little one to his ace. The only difference between West taking spade tricks as declarer and East-West taking spade tricks on defense is that they cannot see each other's hands. But the principle is the same: *The high card(s) from the short side.*

If the defender (East) has four or more cards in partner's suit he returns his original fourth best card.

DUMMY

♠ 7 6 3

WEST   EAST

♠ K J 8 2   ♠ A 10 6 4

SOUTH

♠ Q 9

In this case West would lead the deuce, and East would play the ace and return the *four*—his original fourth best card. Once again, there is a good reason for this as it enables your partner to know how many cards you started with and to work out how many declarer had as well.

Let's have another quiz. This time, sitting East, you must decide not only which card to play at trick one but also which card to return.

DUMMY

♠ 8 4

WEST   EAST (you)

♠ 3   (a)   ♠ Q J 5 2
            (b)   ♠ A 9 7
            (c)   ♠ K 10 6 5 2
            (d)   ♠ A J 5
            (e)   ♠ K Q J
            (f)   ♠ K Q J 10

Solutions

(a) You should play the jack (lower of touching equals) and return the two (original fourth best).

(b) Win the ace and return the nine. (With two remaining cards, return the higher one.)

(c) Play the king and return the five (original fourth best). Notice that the terms fourth best and fourth highest are used interchangeably.

(d) Win the ace and return the jack, as in (b).

(e) Play the jack and return the king, as in (b) and (d).

(f) Play the ten and return the king. (This one is a little different. When you have a complete sequence and you have already played your lowest card then you should return your highest.)

Now, move back into the West position where you are going to have to figure out not only who has the missing honors but also how many cards each player started with in the suit you have led:

(a)

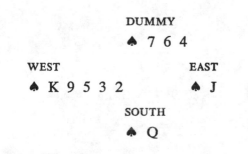

DUMMY
♠ 7 6 4

WEST
♠ K 9 5 3 2

EAST
♠ J

SOUTH
♠ Q

You lead the three of spades and your partner plays the jack, which loses to the queen. Who has the ace and the ten?

(b)

DUMMY
♠ 7 6

WEST
♠ K 10 5 3

EAST
♠ Q

SOUTH
♠ A

You lead the three of spades and your partner plays the queen, which loses to the ace. Who has the jack? Later on your partner regains the lead and returns the deuce of spades. How many spades do you figure your partner had originally?

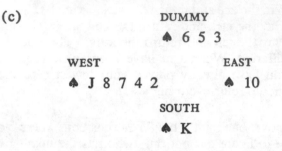

(c)   DUMMY
                       ♠ 6 5 3

       WEST   EAST
       ♠ J 8 7 4 2   ♠ 10

                       SOUTH
                       ♠ K

You lead the four of spades and your partner plays the ten, which loses to the king. Account for all the missing cards!

(d)   DUMMY
                       ♠ 8 4

       WEST   EAST
       ♠ K 9 7 6 3 2   ♠ A

                       SOUTH
                       ♠ 5

You lead the six of spades and partner wins the ace and returns the ten. Declarer plays the queen. Who has the jack?

Solutions

(a)   South has both the ace and the ten. If partner had held the ace and the jack he would have played the ace first, and if partner had held the ten he would have played it in preference to the jack (lower equal).

(b)   South must have the jack because partner's play of the queen has denied it. It might be well to say here

that whichever card partner plays to the first trick
when you lead low and dummy plays low denies the
card directly beneath in rank, but does not deny the
card directly above in rank. This is so important that
it is worth digressing a moment to this:

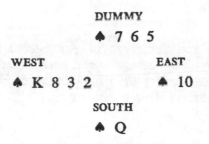

DUMMY

♠ 7 6 5

WEST   **EAST**

♠ K 8 3 2   ♠ 10

SOUTH

♠ Q

West leads the two of spades and partner plays the
ten, which loses to the queen. West knows that East
does not have the nine but cannot be sure about the
jack. Either East or South might hold the jack. After
all, South might have elected to take the first trick
with the queen while holding both the queen and the
jack. The point is that declarer has no rules that he
must follow when taking a trick. He does his best to
try and confuse the defenders. The defenders, on the
other hand, do their best to try and tell each other
exactly what they have. Even with all this honesty
it is not always possible for a defender to pinpoint
the location of a particular honor if declarer happens
to be clever enough to know that it is to his advantage
to win a trick with the higher of *equal* honors.

(c)   Your partner has a singleton ten and South has the
A K Q 9. No other possibility exists. Remember that
your partner's play of the ten has denied the nine,
and if he had held the ace or queen along with the
ten he would have played it. Neither the ace and ten
nor the queen and ten constitute equal honors, and
the higher one must be played in such cases.

(d)   Declarer has the jack. If your partner had had the

A J 10 he would have returned the jack. (With two cards remaining in your partner's suit always return the higher one.) Hopefully you can see that the best way to remember these several rules is to play at every opportunity. These plays come up so many times on each hand that they become habit in no time. The trick is to play.

Now that you think you have mastered third-hand play, consider that in all the cases covered here so far the dummy had two or three little cards. What happens when there is an honor card in the dummy? This brings us to:

THIRD-HAND PLAY WITH AN HONOR CARD IN DUMMY

When there is an honor card in dummy there are two possibilities: (1) Third hand has no honor higher than dummy's, or (2) third hand has an honor higher than dummy's. Let's take the first case because it is the easiest:

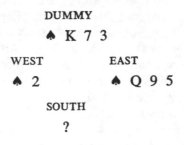

DUMMY

♠ K 7 3

WEST   EAST

♠ 2   ♠ Q 9 5

SOUTH

?

West leads the two, dummy plays the three, and East should *play the queen—the same card he would have played if dummy had no honor cards at all.* In other words, when third hand has no honor card higher than dummy's he plays exactly as if dummy had no honor at all.

But now look at

DUMMY

♠ Q 8 3

WEST   EAST

♠ 2   ♠ A J 4

SOUTH

?

If West leads low and dummy plays low, what should East play now? East should play the jack! Before remembering a rule, look at the entire suit.

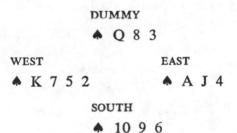

DUMMY

♠ Q 8 3

WEST   EAST

♠ K 7 5 2   ♠ A J 4

SOUTH

♠ 10 9 6

Notice that if East plays the jack he takes the trick; the defense can take three tricks in spades if the hand is played at a suit contract, and four tricks if the hand is played at notrump. East would return first the ace, then the four to West's king. In notrump, West's seven would then be good.

If East takes the first trick with the ace and returns the suit to West's king, dummy's queen stands up for the third trick. Clearly it is better to play the jack the first time.

Perhaps you are wondering how East knows that West has the king. East cannot be completely sure, but West's lead of a low card does promise an honor card, and the only honor cards missing are the king and the ten. Let's take a look to see what would happen if South had the king:

DUMMY

♠ Q 7 3

WEST   EAST

♠ 10 9 5 2   ♠ A J 4

SOUTH

♠ K 8 6

West leads the two, dummy plays low and East plays the jack but South takes the trick with the king. Has anything gone wrong? No. Holding the king and queen in the suit, South is always entitled to one trick. However, if East had played the ace the first time, South would make two tricks—the king *and* the queen!

This is what the suit looks like after East has played the jack:

DUMMY

♠ Q 7

WEST   EAST

♠ 10 9 5   ♠ A 4

SOUTH

♠ 8 6

If *West* gets the lead later in the hand he can lead his ten, and East can capture the queen with the ace. Notice that if *East* should ever get the lead (in another suit) he should not lay down his ace. That will make the queen in dummy high. East must wait for West to lead through the queen. If the defense plays properly it will take at least two tricks by playing the jack the first time rather than only one by playing the ace.

Take a look at this hand to see third-hand play in action:

DUMMY

♠ K 4 3
♡ Q J 7 5
◊ A J 10 9
♣ Q 4

WEST

♠ 9 8 7 6
♡ 6 2
◊ 8 7 6 3
♣ A J 2

EAST

♠ A J 10
♡ 9 3
◊ K 5 2
♣ 9 8 7 6 5

SOUTH

♠ Q 6 5
♡ A K 10 8 4
◊ Q 4
♣ K 10 3

South plays in a contract of 4 ♡*. West leads the nine of spades (top of nothing). Dummy plays low, and the fate of the entire hand depends upon the card that East plays to this trick! If East plays the ten (not the jack because the jack and the ten are equals and the defenders always play the lower equal) South wins the queen. South removes the trumps and winds up in his own hand.

In an effort to rid himself of his losing spades, South finesses the queen of diamonds to East, who wins the king. At this point East has the ace and the jack of spades and dummy the king and the four. If East lays down his ace of spades, dummy's king becomes good. In order to make two tricks in spades East must put West in to lead through dummy's king.

The only hope is clubs. East leads the nine (top of nothing) and West takes the trick with the ace. West now returns a spade, knowing that East has nothing in clubs and seeing that the diamonds are established, and East makes both the jack and the

* The rules for third-hand play apply both to notrump and to suit contracts.

ace to defeat the contract. Had East played his ace of spades to the first trick, South would have lost only one spade trick and made his contract.

You can see how important it is for third hand to make the proper plays. The rule that third hand follows when he has an honor higher than dummy's is simply this:

If dummy has an honor card (jack, queen, or king) and third hand has a *higher honor,* third hand plays as follows:

(1)   if the honor is played from dummy, third hand covers dummy's honor.

(2)   if the honor in dummy is not played, third hand keeps his honor and plays his next highest card, provided it is a *nine* or better.

Let's take a look at each case:

```
                    DUMMY
                   ♠ Q 7 4
        WEST                EAST
         ♠ 2               ♠ K 9 3
                    SOUTH
                      ?
```

West leads the two and dummy plays the queen. East would cover with the king. If dummy plays low, East would save the king—holding it over the queen—and play the nine instead.

Now picture the same diagram assuming that East started with K 8 3. If dummy plays low East would play the king. If third hand is to retain his honor card over dummy he must be able to insert a nine or higher. If he cannot, he plays his honor card. This calls for a little practice.

Assume you are always East and your partner leads the two.

DUMMY

♠ K 7 3

WEST	EAST		
♠ 2	(a)	♠	A Q 9
	(b)	♠	Q 10 5
	(c)	♠	A J 9
	(d)	♠	A 6 4
	(e)	♠	Q J 10 4
	(f)	♠	A J 10 9
	(g)	♠	A 10 8
	(h)	♠	J 9

SOUTH

?

Assuming dummy plays low, which card should East play?

Solutions

(a) The queen   Common sense should tell you this. The queen is as good as the ace, with the king in the dummy.

(b) The queen   When dummy has an honor higher than your highest you simply play third hand as if there were no honor in the dummy at all.

(c) The jack   Retain the higher honor over dummy's honor and play the next highest card as long as it is the nine or better.

(d) The ace   You have no card as high as the nine to play.

(e) The ten   Lowest of three touching equals.

(f) The nine   The jack, ten, and nine are all equals, and you must save the ace to catch the king so you play the nine, the lowest of touching equals.

(g) The ten   Save the ace to capture the king.

(h) The jack   Third hand high when dummy has an honor higher than your highest.

There will also be times like this:

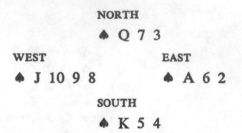

NORTH

♠ Q 7 3

WEST   EAST

♠ J 10 9 8   ♠ A 6 2

SOUTH

♠ K 5 4

West leads the jack and dummy plays low. What should East do? He should simply signal with the six.

South wins the king, but if the defense plays properly that will be South's only trick. Had East played the ace, South would have made both the king and the queen.

We can now say this: If partner leads an *honor card*, dummy has a higher honor, and third hand has an honor higher than dummy's, third hand should play his honor only if dummy plays its honor.

Unfortunately, not one of these rules is as good as a little common sense.

Look at this case:

NORTH

♠ K 3 2
♡ Q J 10 9
◇ A K Q J
♣ 7 6

WEST   EAST

♠ J 10 9 8 7 6   ♠ A 5 4
♡ 2   ♡ A 3
◇ 10 9 8 7   ◇ 6 5 4
♣ 5 4   ♣ J 9 8 3 2

SOUTH

♠ Q
♡ K 8 7 6 5 4
◇ 3 2
♣ A K Q 10

Through a bidding misunderstanding South winds up playing a contract of six hearts and West leads the jack of spades. Dummy plays low and East must win the ace.

East must keep sight of the most important thing of all—the contract. East has the slam defeated by taking his ace of spades (it can't be trumped because, based on partner's lead of the jack, South must have the queen) and waiting to play his ace of trump. In other words, logic, common sense, and the contract dictate that East must win the first trick with the ace of spades rather than waiting for the king to be played.

You cannot be a robot and expect to be a good bridge player. At first, you should follow the rules just to keep the game going, but eventually you are going to have to *think*.

There is still another important addition to third-hand play:

UNBLOCKING BY THIRD HAND

Consider this common notrump situation:

DUMMY

♠ 7 5 3

WEST   EAST

♠ K Q J 8 4   ♠ A 2

SOUTH

♠ 10 9 6

South plays a notrump contract and West leads the king. Which card should East play? East must play the ace!

This play is not so wild as it seems. Remember that the lead of the king shows either K Q J or K Q 10, and if East, holding a doubleton, does not play the ace, he will win the second trick but will be unable to return the suit.

Let's see what happens when East plays the ace. He returns the two, and West takes the remaining four tricks in the suit. In other words, East saves three tricks by putting his ace on his partner's king!

What you must see is this: When you have a doubleton ace you must unblock for your partner's greater length. Remember the high card from the short side when you are taking tricks in a suit? Well, this is the principle. The defense also plays the high card from the short side when it is taking tricks.

Now let's look at another unblocking play:

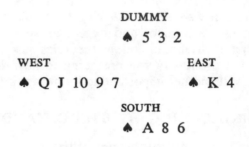

DUMMY

♠ 5 3 2

WEST   EAST

♠ Q J 10 9 7   ♠ K 4

SOUTH

♠ A 8 6

South plays a notrump contract and West leads the queen. South has only one spade stopper and does not want to relinquish it if he can help it. If East and South play low, West can continue the suit to East's king. Let's say South plays low again. East has no more spades and the defense cannot remove South's only spade stopper.

Let's see what happens if East makes the correct play of the king on partner's queen. South plays low and East continues the suit. South plays the eight, but this time West wins the second round of the suit and can drive out South's ace.

East should not think in terms of "wasting honors" when he puts the king on the queen. He should think of the necessity of driving out South's ace, and if he doesn't put the king on the queen the defense will be unable to remove South's only stopper.

These two unblocking plays occur at both notrump and suit contracts and your partner is sure to be impressed when you make them.

KEY POINTERS

(1)   Third-hand play to the first trick is one of the most important facets of defensive play.

(2)   Third hand must always consider the contract, look at the card partner is leading and at the dummy before deciding which card to play.

(3)   If partner leads a low card it announces the possession of an honor card. The lead of an honor card shows a sequence. The lead of a high middle card (eight or nine) is usually top of nothing. The lead of the nine is always the opening leader's highest card in the suit.

(4)   If partner leads a low card and dummy comes down with low cards in the suit, third hand must play his highest card. If third hand's highest card has one or two equals he must play the lower or the lowest equal (the jack from queen-jack or the ten from queen-jack-ten).

(5)   It is also important for third hand to know which card to *return* in partner's suit. With *two remaining* cards, return the *higher*. With *three* remaining cards, return the *lowest*. With *four or more* remaining cards return your *original fourth best* card. With A 8 7 5 3 win the ace and return the five.

(6)   If you play your cards in the proper order, your partner, who has made the opening lead, can tell where the missing honors are and how many cards each player originally held in that particular suit.

(7)   When dummy comes down with an honor card and third hand has a higher honor, third hand normally saves its honor until dummy's honor has been played, inserting his next highest card instead (if it is as good as the nine).

(8)   If partner leads an honor card, dummy has a higher honor, and third hand has a still higher honor, third hand waits for dummy's honor to be played.

(9)   If third hand has a doubleton ace or a doubleton king he usually plays his honor on top of partner's honor lead. This is called unblocking and is done to help partner set up his long suit.

(10)   In all cases of third-hand play common sense overrides all rules.

Common sense in action:

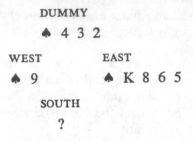

DUMMY

♠ 4 3 2

WEST   EAST

♠ 9   ♠ K 8 6 5

SOUTH

?

West leads the nine, which must be his highest card. East should not play the king because he knows that South has the A Q J 10.

(11)   Watch dummy's cards closely!

DUMMY

♠ A J 6 2

WEST   EAST (you)

♠ 5   ♠ Q 10 9 7

SOUTH

?

West leads the five and dummy plays the deuce. East should play the nine. With the jack in the dummy, the queen, ten, and nine are all equal cards. East is simply playing his lowest equal. Had there been no jack in the dummy East would play the queen.

(12)   For practical purposes, third-hand play against suit contracts is similar to third-hand play against notrump. However, one must remember that against notrump the opening leader is apt to lead from his longest suit, whereas against a suit contract he will often be leading from a short suit.

3

Signaling vs. Notrump

♠ ♡ ◇ ♣

If you have read this far in the book you have probably played some bridge by now. Assuming you have played some, it is a virtual certainty that the most confusing part of the game for you is defense. This is the case with many players.

Even an expert will make more mistakes on defense than in any other phase of the game. But, and this is important, if you sit an expert down opposite a partner who does not know the fundamentals of third-hand play and signaling, the expert is quite likely to make a mistake or two on every hand!

This underscores the fact that bridge is a partnership game. If you know more about defensive play than does your partner, you had better teach him what you know. Otherwise, his bad plays are going to cause you to make mistakes!

One of the best methods of conveying information about your hand to your partner is by means of signals—legal ones. There are certain standard defensive signals that are used the world over. Without them bridge can become little more than a guessing game.

What are these signals? In this chapter we will discuss some defensive signals and save the remainder for the chapter on Signaling vs. Suit Contracts.

THE COUNT SIGNAL

In order to understand the importance of the "count signal" you must look at the following two deals that South plays in 3 NT.

(1)   NORTH
                       ♠ 7 6 3
                       ♡ 7 2
                       ◇ K Q J 10 4
                       ♣ 9 4 3

WEST   EAST
♠ Q 9 4 2   ♠ J 10 8
♡ J 9   ♡ Q 10 8 7 6
◇ 6 3 2   ◇ A 9 5
♣ J 8 6 5   ♣ 10 9

                       SOUTH
                       ♠ A K 5
                       ♡ A K 5 4
                       ◇ 8 7
                       ♣ A K Q 2

West leads a low spade, East plays the ten (lower of
equals), and South wins the king. As you can see, South has
seven sure tricks outside the diamond suit, which is his best suit
in the combined hands.

Let's see what happens if South leads a diamond now. West
plays low and dummy plays the king. If East takes the trick,
South will remain with another diamond and will be able to take
four more diamond tricks and make his contract easily.

But what if East does not take the trick? What if East takes
the second diamond instead of the first? South will have no way
of getting to dummy's diamonds and will make only one diamond trick instead of four, thus being defeated one trick.

But wait a minute! What if East decided to take the third
diamond? Then South would make his contract, because he
would have made two tricks in diamonds. Clearly, it is right for
East to take precisely the second diamond, because South has

only two diamonds. If South had three diamonds, then East should take the third diamond. How can East tell?

Before the answer look at this deal:

(2)   NORTH
                         ♠ 7 6 3 2
                         ♡ 7 2
                         ◊ K Q J 10
                         ♣ 9 4 3

WEST   EAST
♠ J 9 8   ♠ Q 10 5 4
♡ Q J 10 6   ♡ 9 8 5
◊ 8 2   ◊ A 9 5 4
♣ J 8 7 6   ♣ Q 10

                         SOUTH
                         ♠ A K
                         ♡ A K 4 3
                         ◊ 7 6 3
                         ♣ A K 5 2

This time West leads the queen of hearts against South's 3 NT. South has six sure tricks and must try to set up the diamonds.

Let's say South leads a diamond at trick two. If East takes the ace South will have established three tricks in diamonds and will make his game contract. In fact, if East takes the second diamond, which was the correct play on the previous hand, South will still make his contract, because South will have a third diamond with which to get to dummy.

On this particular hand East must take the *third* diamond to defeat the contract. By taking the third diamond East will hold South to two diamond tricks. But how does East know to take the second diamond on the first deal and the third diamond on the second deal?

Simple. *West* has told East which diamond to take—not in words, but with a count signal.

Before a discussion of the count signal you must see this: Whenever declarer is setting up a long suit in dummy and there are no side entries to the suit the defender with the ace must win the trick at the same time declarer is playing his *last* card in dummy's long suit.

This means that if declarer started with one card in dummy's suit the defender with the ace should take the first trick. If the declarer started with two cards the defender should take the second trick and so on. In this manner the declarer will be prevented from getting over to dummy to use the rest of the tricks in that suit.

Now let's take another look at both of these deals. In the first deal South led a diamond at trick two and West, who is the key man in this operation, must tell East how many diamonds he has. Once East can figure out how many diamonds West has, he can figure out how many diamonds South has and thus know which diamond trick to win.

When using the count signal (whenever declarer is establishing dummy's long suit) the defender with three small cards must play his *lowest card first*. With two small cards the defender must play his *highest card first*. For the time being we will not worry about the defender having four or five small cards although it can't hurt to know that with four small cards the defender plays his second highest and then his lowest, and with five small cards his lowest first.

On deal one West must play his deuce of diamonds, his lowest card in the suit, to show East an original holding of three diamonds. East can then figure out that if West started with three diamonds South must have started with two; thus, he can confidently win the second diamond trick.

Now take a look at the second deal. When South leads a diamond at trick two, West must play the eight of diamonds to show East a doubleton. East can then figure by looking at his own diamond holding and dummy's how many diamonds South has. In this case East can figure that South has three and can confidently win the third trick, shutting declarer out of dummy's fourth diamond.

Let's do a little practicing:

DUMMY

◇ K Q J 10

WEST		EAST
(a) ◇ 7 3		?
(b) ◇ 8 7 2		
(c) ◇ 9 6 5		
(d) ◇ 9 5		

DECLARER

◇ 4

Let's say you are defending a notrump contract (the count signal is the same at a suit contract) and declarer leads the four of diamonds up to dummy's strength. Which diamond should you play?

In the first and last cases (a and d) you should play your higher diamond. In the middle two cases (b and c) you should play your lowest diamond. In this way your partner will be able to tell which diamond to take with his presumed ace. If declarer has the ace it won't matter which diamond you play, but since you don't know who has it you must presume it is your partner.

Incidentally, you would give the same count signal if you were East and declarer were leading up to dummy:

DUMMY

◇ K Q J 10

WEST	EAST
◇ 3	◇ 8 7
	◇ 6 5 2

DECLARER

◇ 4

In this case West might have the ace and be waiting to see which diamond you play so he will know which one to take with his ace. In the first case you should play the eight and in the second the two.

Now let's see how good you are at reading your partner's count signal.

DUMMY

◊ K Q J 10

WEST   EAST (you)

◊ 3   ◊ A 8 7 5

DECLARER

◊ 2

Declarer leads the deuce of diamonds and partner plays the three. How many diamonds does the *Declarer* have and which diamond should you plan to take?

Partner is playing his lowest diamond so he must have three; that leaves declarer with two diamonds, so you should take the second round of diamonds with your ace.

Try this:

DUMMY

◊ K Q J 10 9

WEST   EAST (you)

◊ 8   ◊ A 7 4

DECLARER

◊ 2

Declarer leads the deuce, partner plays the eight. Which one do you plan to take?

You should figure your partner for a doubleton and that leaves declarer with three cards in the suit. So you should take the third diamond lead.

There are a few other pointers about this count signal. The player with the ace does not have to give his partner the count, but the player with the small cards must give his partner the count.

If there is a side entry to the dummy the count signal loses some of its effectiveness, but it should still be given.

The count signal is used primarily when declarer is setting up dummy's long suit. Of course, the long suit does not always have K Q J 10. It might look like this:

DUMMY

◊ Q J 10 9

WEST   EAST

◊ 8 2   ◊ A 7 6 5

SOUTH

◊ K 4 3

South leads the king and West plays the eight. East now can count West for a doubleton and win the third round of diamonds. The play would be the same if the East and West cards were reversed.

Here's a tricky application of the count signal:

DUMMY

◊ A Q J 10 9

WEST   EAST

◊ 7 6 2   ◊ K 8 3

SOUTH

◊ 5 4

South leads the five and West plays the deuce, showing three cards in diamonds. East can now deduce that South has two diamonds. Assuming South finesses the queen of diamonds East should play low! South will probably think that West has the king and return to his hand to repeat the finesse; he is in store for a shock. When South finesses the diamond a second time East wins the king and South may never be able to use the remainder of dummy's diamonds.

Notice that if East had taken the first diamond with the king, South would have another diamond to get over to dummy's good tricks.

THE EQUAL HONOR SIGNAL

In order to appreciate the advantages of the equal honor signal, one must simply try to defend a few hands without it. For example:

DUMMY

♠ 7 6 3

WEST   EAST

♠ Q J 10 9   ?

SOUTH

♠ A

Assume that you are West and you lead the queen of spades against a notrump contract. Declarer takes the trick with the ace. Who has the king?

The truth of the matter is the only way you can tell is by the card your partner plays to the first trick. If your partner has an honor *equal* to the one that you have led he should signal you by playing the highest card under his honor that he can afford. For example:

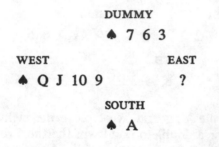

DUMMY

♠ 7 6 3

WEST   EAST

♠ Q   ♠ K 8 2

                                        ♠ K 8 5 4

                                        ♠ K 8

                                        ♠ 8 2

                                        ♠ 8 5 4

                                        ♠ 8 5 4 2

DECLARER

?

Assume that you are East and your partner has led the queen of spades against a notrump contract. Dummy plays low and you have each of the above holdings in spades. How would you inform your partner as to your holding?

Keep in mind that your partner is interested mainly in one thing: Do you have an honor card in the suit he has led?

In the first two cases, holding an equal honor you would play the eight under partner's queen. *Whenever partner leads an honor card and you play a rather high middle card you are normally telling your partner that you have an equal honor in his suit.*

What is the definition of a rather high middle card? Unfortunately it may be as low as the three! What if you have K 3 2? The highest card you can afford is the three. Similarly with K 4 3 2 the best you can give your partner is the four. However, most of the time you will have a slightly bigger card, and partner will be able to tell that you are signaling.

A very clever partner will even be able to read a three or four as a *possible signal* because the lower cards that you are holding will not be visible. As long as your partner has reason to believe you are not playing your lowest card, he has reason to believe that you may be signaling.

Back to our original diagram, with the K 8 East must play the king! Remember that if you have a doubleton honor you must unblock with the king. Review the lesson on third-hand play if you have forgotten why.

With the other three holdings you have no honor card in partner's suit and you should play your *lowest* spade. Using the equal honor signal will usually allow partner to figure out who has what.

There are two cases in which the equal honor signal may be a little confusing. The first appears in this common situation:

DUMMY

♠ 6 5 3

WEST   EAST

♠ Q   ♠ 10 7 2

SOUTH

♠ ?

West leads the queen of spades. Which spade should East play? The important point to realize is that West has both the queen and jack, and the ten is actually equal to the queen! Therefore, when partner leads the queen and you have the ten you should begin a signal with the seven. Indeed the ten is such an important card that if you hold 10 x you must drop the ten under partner's queen as a form of unblocking play, at the same time showing your partner the ten. The play of the ten under the queen will not cost a trick because partner must be leading from Q J 9. If partner did not have Q J 9 he would have led fourth highest in the suit.

The most common—slightly different—equal honor situation arises in this familiar position:

```
           DUMMY
           ♠ 6 4

 WEST      EAST
 ♠ K       ♠ A 8 3 2    Q 8 3 2    J 8 3 2    9 8 3 2
           ♠ A 8 2      Q 8 2      J 8 2      9 8 2
           ♠ A 8        Q 8        J 8        8 2

           SOUTH
             ?
```

Partner leads the king against a notrump contract. First let's consider your play holding the ace—an equal honor. With A 8 3 2 or A 8 2 you should signal with the eight. With the A 8 you should overtake the king with the ace.

With Q 8 3 2, or Q 8 2 you should play the eight because you have an equal honor. With the Q 8 you should also play the eight. If your partner had wanted to force you to throw away your queen he would have led the ace. (See Chapter 1, "The Opening Lead.")

When partner leads the king, the jack is considered an equal honor. Therefore, with J 8 3 2 and J 8 2 East should signal with the eight. With the J 8 doubleton East must unblock the jack. This might appear to be contradictory, but you unblock the jack

for the same reason you unblock the ten from a doubleton ten
when partner leads the queen. The lead of the king will usually
be from K Q J or K Q 10. When you have the jack, partner
must have K Q 10, and your play will help clarify the position
for him. (In all the other cases where you have no equal honor
you should simply play your lowest card.)

In order to see what you have learned, put yourself in the
West seat and try to figure out what is going on. Keep in mind
that partner will be signaling you if he has an equal honor.

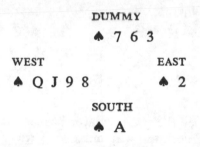

DUMMY

♠ 7 6 3

WEST   EAST

♠ Q J 9 8   ♠ 2

SOUTH

♠ A

You lead the queen and partner plays the deuce. Declarer
wins the ace. Who has the king and who has the ten?

Declarer must have them both. If partner had either the ten
or the king he would have started a signal. He has played his
lowest card indicating that he has no equal honor in your suit.

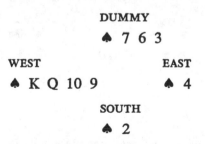

DUMMY

♠ 7 6 3

WEST   EAST

♠ K Q 10 9   ♠ 4

SOUTH

♠ 2

You lead the king, partner plays the four, and declarer the
two. Do you continue the suit?

You had better not! Declarer is working one of the oldest

tricks in the book on you; he is executing a sneaky little play known as the "Bath Coup." You see, declarer must have both the ace and the jack. Your partner can't have either, since he played the four—which you recognize as his lowest card because you can see the two and three. So why isn't declarer taking your king? Look at this and you will see why:

DUMMY

♠ 7 6 3

WEST   EAST

♠ K Q 10 9   ♠ 8 5 4

SOUTH

♠ A J 2

Can you see the trap declarer has set for you? If you play another spade, declarer will make two tricks in the suit. You must simply shift suits and wait for your partner to lead a spade through the declarer's ace-jack. Without the equal honor signal you would never know to shift suits.

How about this one?

DUMMY

♠ 5 2

WEST   EAST

♠ K Q 10 4   ♠ 8

SOUTH

♠ 3

You lead the king, partner plays the eight, and declarer the three. What do you think?

Partner's play of the eight indicates either the ace or the jack, or both. In any case it is safe to lead your four, as partner will protect your low card by playing his honor. In fact this could have been the entire distribution:

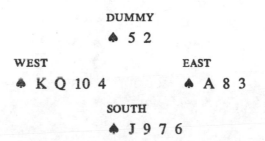

DUMMY

♠ 5 2

WEST   EAST

♣ K Q 10 4   ♠ A 8 3

SOUTH

♠ J 9 7 6

By your leading the four the second time to your partner's ace he can return his three and you will take the next two tricks with your queen and ten.

Once you have mastered the equal honor signal you must be aware of its counterpart, the unequal honor signal.

This occurs when you have an honor that is higher but not an equal to the honor your partner has led. The first and most common is:

DUMMY

♠ 7 6 3

WEST   EAST

♠ Q   ♠ A 8 2

SOUTH

?

Defending a notrump contract, East knows that South has the guarded king and normally signals with the eight spot, as it is impossible to prevent South from taking at least one trick with his king.

At a *suit* contract East would play the *ace*, as there is a possibility that South has a singleton king!

We also have this:

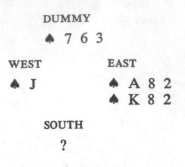

The lead of the jack can be from J 10 9, J 10 8, A J 10, or
K J 10.

Because of the last two possibilities East is obliged to play
his high honor when his partner leads the jack.

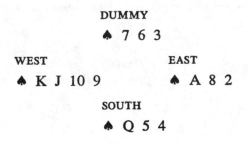

It would be embarrassing for East and West to allow South
to take a trick with the queen in this case. With, again, the jack
lead, if East plays the ace and returns the eight (higher of two
remaining cards) South cannot take a single trick in the suit. If
we switch the ace and king in the East-West hands, the lead
would be the same and East would have to play the king over
his partner's jack.

Finally, we have cases where partner leads the ten and we
have either the queen, king, or ace.

Study this:

DUMMY

♠ 7 6 3

WEST   EAST

♠ K 10 9 8   ♠ Q 5 4

SOUTH

♠ A J 2

West leads the ten (remember that the ten is led from A 10 9, K 10 9, or Q 10 9 as well as from 10 9 8 or 10 9 7) and East must play the queen or South will take a cheap trick with the jack.

The same would be true if the queen and king were exchanged in the East-West hands.

Now, for a short quiz:

DUMMY

♠ 7 6 2

WEST   EAST

♠ J   ♠ K 8 5

                  ♠ Q 8 5

                  ♠ A 5 4

                  ♠ 8 3

SOUTH

?

Which card should East play on partner's lead of the jack?

(a) With K 8 5, East should cover with the king because West might be leading from A J 10.

(b) With Q 8 5, East should signal with the eight because he has an equal honor.

(c) With A 5 4, East should play the ace because West might be leading from K J 10.

(d)   With 8 3, East should play the three because he has no honor in partner's suit.

SUMMARY OF THIRD-HAND PLAY
WHEN PARTNER LEADS AN HONOR

(1)   If partner leads the ace, drop any high honor you may have. (With no high honor play your smallest card if you have three and your top card if you have two.)

(2)   If partner leads the king, signal if you hold the ace, queen, or jack. Overtake if you have doubleton ace and unblock if you have a doubleton jack.

(3)   If partner leads the queen, signal if you hold the ace, king, or ten. Overtake with the doubleton king or doubleton ace. Unblock with the doubleton ten.

(4)   If partner leads the jack, signal if you hold the queen. Overtake with the king or ace provided dummy has no honor cards in the suit.

(5)   If partner leads the ten, signal if you hold the jack. Overtake with the queen, king, or ace if dummy has no honor cards in the suit.

(6)   If partner leads an honor and you have no honor cards in the suit at all, play your smallest card.

THE DISCARD SIGNAL

Many times at notrump either your partner or the declarer will be playing a suit in which you have no more cards. In these cases you must make a discard (or a sluff), and the discards you make can show either strength or weakness. Basically, there are two types of discard signals:

(1) A high discard indicates strength in the suit being discarded. For example: if you were going to discard from A K 8 5 2 and you wanted to let partner know about your strength you would discard the eight. This is known as a positive signal.

(2) A low discard indicates weakness in the suit being discarded. This is known as a negative signal; for example, discarding the deuce from 8 3 2.

Very often it will be difficult to determine whether partner is making a positive or a negative signal from seeing only one card. However, if he gets a chance to make a second discard in the same suit he can usually clear up this confusion.

A high-low discard in the same suit shows strength. Therefore, a discard of the four followed by the deuce indicates strength in the suit. A low-high discard in the same suit, such as the seven followed by the eight, indicates weakness.

Naturally, it is easier to decide which signal your partner is making after you see two cards. but you don't always have that luxury.

Is it better to make positive or negative signals? Logic should tell you that negative signals are better at notrump, because you can then save all of your cards in your best suit. For example, assume that you must select between discarding from the A K 10 8 of spades or the 4 3 2 of hearts and you can make only one discard.

You should not waste any of your good spades (the A K 10 8 suit) but should discard the two of hearts (your 4 3 2 suit). The two of hearts is just as emphatic a denial as the eight or ten would be an encouragement, and you retain all your good cards.

Two Negative Signals Equals One Positive Signal!

DUMMY
♠ 8 7 5 3
♡ J 8 4
◊ A J 10
♣ K 6 5

WEST   EAST
♠ A 9 6 4 2   ♠ ——
♡ 7 3   ♡ A K Q 10
◊ 8 7 4   ◊ 9 6 5 3 2
♣ 10 9 7   ♣ 8 4 3 2

SOUTH
♠ K Q J 10
♡ 9 6 5 2
◊ K Q
♣ A Q J

South plays 3 NT and West leads the four of spades. South wins with an honor, and East discards the two of diamonds, showing no interest in diamonds. At this point West knows that South started with K Q J 10 of spades as East is void.

South decides to establish his spades and returns one.

On the second round of spades West wins the ace and East discards the two of clubs, showing no interest in clubs. Now it is easy for West to shift to the seven of hearts. East then can run off *four* heart tricks and defeat the contract one trick. Had East wasted the ten of hearts in order to make a positive signal the defense could have taken only three heart tricks and the contract would have been made.

KEY POINTERS

(1) When declarer begins establishing his long suit in dummy, the defender with weakness in dummy's long suit must

give his partner a count signal. He does this by playing his lowest card if he has three cards and the top card if he has a doubleton.

(2) When partner leads an honor card and you have an equal honor, you normally signal unless you have a doubleton honor, in which case you unblock by playing your honor.

(3) If partner leads the jack or the ten, you normally cover with the king or ace to protect your partner's holding and to prevent declarer from taking a cheap trick.

(4) If partner leads an honor card and you have no honor card in his suit, play your lowest card.

(5) If you lead an honor card, watch whether your partner, by his play, is beginning an equal honor signal or is warning you that he has no honor cards.

(6) When discarding, keep in mind that there are two types of signals—positive and negative. A positive discard is the discard of a rather high spot-card to indicate strength in the suit discarded. A negative discard is the discard of your smallest card in a suit to indicate weakness.

(7) As a general rule, better players make negative discards against notrump in order to retain their high cards. Beginners are more apt to make positive discards.

(8) By making negative discards in two different suits you are implying strength in a third suit.

(9) A high-low discard in the same suit indicates strength; a low-high discard in the same suit indicates weakness.

(10) Never discard your last card in the suit that your partner has led. You may get the lead and want to play that suit. As a general rule you should never discard down to a void or a singleton in a suit even if you are very weak in that suit. The reason is that when Declarer plays the suit and you have no more he will know immediately what card your partner has and will make all the proper finesses. Try to confine your negative discards to longer weak suits.

(11) Remember—you are trying to give your partner information. Make it simple.

Part II
DEFENSE VS. SUIT CONTRACTS

♠ ♡ ◇ ♣

Your objectives when defending a suit contract are the same as when defending a notrump contract: (1) to defeat the contract, and (2) to give partner information about your hand by proper leads and by signaling.

The main difference between a suit contract and notrump is that at a suit contract it no longer pays the defense to establish long suits, because either the declarer or the dummy will simply trump the tricks that the defense has established.

This affects your choice of opening leads. Against a notrump contract, from A K 7 5 2 you lead the five. You are willing to give up one trick to the declarer in the hopes of getting back four. However, at a suit contract it would be the height of madness to lead the five because either the dummy or the declarer might be short suited and you would never be able to take your ace and king.

Against notrump you are constantly leading long suits in an effort to establish tricks. Against suit contracts you are more apt to be leading short suits (singletons or doubletons) hoping to eventually trump one of declarer's good cards in that suit.

Whatever you lead, partner must be aware of what you have in the suit. For that reason, once you have decided upon the suit you don't just throw a card on the table.

♠ ♡ ◇ ♣

1

The Opening Lead

♠ ♡ ◇ ♣

Basically, once you have decided upon a suit, the card you lead will be the same card you would have led had you been defending a notrump contract—with three exceptions:

(1) From the ace-king. With A K 7 6 4 3, you would lead the six against notrump but the king against a suit contract. The king is always led from A-K combinations against suit contracts.

(2) From the king-queen. With K Q 7 5 3, you would lead the five against notrump but the king against a suit contract. The king is always led from the king-queen against suit contracts. The idea behind the lead is to build up one trick in the suit.

At this point it might be wise to mention that leads from the A K and the K Q are among the strongest to be made against suit contracts. Therefore, you can expect your partner to be leading a king very often. In order to determine whether your partner is leading from A K or K Q simply look at the dummy and your own hand. Almost always you will see either the ace or queen and should be able to work it out. For example: if you have the queen you know partner has the A K. If you see the ace in the dummy you know partner has the K Q. If you see neither the ace nor queen in either your hand or the dummy you simply can't tell which combination partner has.

(3) Suits that contain the ace. Against notrump contracts you lead low (fourth best) from

A 7 6 3   A 8 5 4 3   or   A 7 6 4 3 2

Against suit contracts if you are ever leading a suit that contains the ace, the normal play is to lead the ace.

As a quick review, assume that you are leading against a suit contract. Which card would you lead from each of the following holdings?

(a) K 6 4	(e) A K 7 6 5	(i) Q 7 6 4 3
(b) K Q 6 4	(f) Q 5	(j) Q J 10 4
(c) 8 3	(g) 9 5 3	(k) J 5 3 2
(d) A 7 6 3	(h) K J 4 2	

Solutions

(a)	The four	Low from an honor
(b)	The king	King from king-queen vs. suit; the four vs. notrump
(c)	The eight	Top of a doubleton
(d)	The ace	Against notrump the three
(e)	The king	Against notrump the six (When holding the A K alone against a suit contract, lead the ace and then the king. This tells partner you started with only two cards in the suit.)
(f)	The queen	Top of a doubleton
(g)	The nine	Top of nothing
(h)	The two	Fourth best if you have no sequence
(i)	The four	Fourth best
(j)	The queen	Top of a sequence
(k)	The two	Fourth best

Let's assume that you have memorized these leads and that your problem is to select the suit. How do you figure that out?

The most important point is to *remember the bidding*. Avoid leading your opponent's suit or suits unless you have a sequence or perhaps a singleton. Tend to lead sequences, suits that have the A K or K Q, partner's suit, or unbid suits.

Let's take some examples. You are West and you hear this common bidding sequence:

SOUTH	WEST	NORTH	EAST
1 ♠	Pass	2 ♠	Pass
4 ♠	Pass	Pass	Pass

Now consider this hand:

♠ Q 5   ♡ J 8 7 4   ◇ A K 6 3   ♣ 9 6 4

Your partner has not bid so you are faced with a blind lead. Since the two best leads are sequences or the king from ace-king, you should definitely lead the king of diamonds.

With the same bidding, consider this hand:

♠ 7 6 3   ♡ 2   ◇ A 7 6 4 3   ♣ Q 7 6 4

You have no sequences or A K combinations, and your partner hasn't bid anything so you are on your own. As a general rule a singleton in an unbid suit is a good choice, so you should lead the deuce of hearts.

It should be noted that a beginning player is more apt to lead a singleton than anything else. If partner has the ace he can win the lead and return the suit so that you can make a small trump. That is very true. But always look at your own trump holding before you lead a singleton.

Again, with the same bidding as before, this is your hand:

♠ Q J 10 9   ♡ 2   ◇ A 7 6   ♣ Q 7 6 4 3

You can see that you have two natural tricks in trump whether you trump anything or not. You gain nothing by trumping, and, therefore, should *not* lead a heart.

We have a general rule about leading a short suit (unless, of course, partner has bid it). When holding either "natural trump tricks" or four trumps, do not lead a short suit. With four trumps you normally lead your longest suit. In the above example you might even lead the queen of spades. Had your four spades not been in sequence, however, you would lead the four of clubs.

Let's talk a little more about natural trump tricks. *A*

natural trump trick is a trick that cannot be taken away from you. The best example is Q J 10. You must get one trump trick; if you trump another suit you lose that trick so you merely break even. But what if you have A 3 2 of trumps or K 3 2? In these cases, if you *ruff* (trump) one of declarers' winners with one of your worthless trumps you have promoted an extra trick for your side.

Consider this layout of the trump suit:

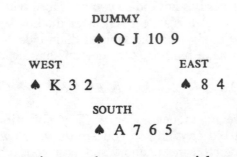

DUMMY

♠ Q J 10 9

WEST   EAST

♠ K 3 2   ♠ 8 4

SOUTH

♠ A 7 6 5

West is certain to make one trump trick, and if West can trump something with a small trump he will make two trump tricks. Therefore, with K x x or A x x in trumps a short suit lead is particularly effective.

However, with four trumps one does not normally lead a short suit. Your most effective defense in this case is to lead your *longest suit!* The idea behind this lead is to force the declarer to trump, hoping that you will soon have as many or more trumps than he. When this happens, the declarer can kiss his contract goodbye. It is next to impossible for him to retain control of a hand when a defender has more trumps than he does.

In the light of this discussion, what would you lead from each of the following hands against the same bidding?

SOUTH	NORTH
1 ♠	2 ♠
4 ♠	Pass

You are West:

(a) ♠ A 6 5   ♡ K 7 6 3   ◊ Q 7 6 3   ♣ 7 2
(b) ♠ K 8 5 3   ♡ K 7 6 3 2   ◊ Q 2   ♣ 7 2

(c) ♠ Q J 6   ♡ 8 3   ◊ Q J 10 4   ♣ K 5 4 2
(d) ♠ A 9 3 2   ♡ 8 3   ◊ Q 10 6 4 2   ♣ J 5

Solutions

(a) The seven of clubs   With A x x or K x x of trumps, a short suit lead is very desirable.

(b) The three of hearts   With four trumps, lead your longest suit.

(c) The queen of diamonds   You have a natural trump trick and there is no need to try for a ruff.

(d) The four of diamonds   With four trumps, lead your longest suit.

It might be well to digress a moment to mention that whenever you play bridge, as if by magic, at least one player at the table will become the "teacher."

You are very lucky if you have a good teacher at every game, but most are apt to give you some bad advice. For example, I am sure you have heard someone say "Never lead away from a king," or "When in doubt lead trumps."

Unfortunately, these little sayings are not true. It is safer to lead away from a king than from a queen or jack. For example, if you lead away from a queen and the opponents have the ace-king-jack, you will never take a trick in the suit. If you lead away from a king, you might still get a trick even if the opponents have the ace-queen-jack.

                         DUMMY
                         ♠ 5 4 3

        WEST   EAST
        ♠ K 10 6 2   ♠ 9 8 7

                         SOUTH
                         ♠ A Q J

Let's say you (West) lead the two of spades and declarer wins the jack or queen. Most of the time, you will still make your king. Besides, you are very unlucky that your partner doesn't have either the queen or the ace.

Two of the times when you should go out of your way to lead from a king are when you have four trumps and your longest suit contains a king, or when your longest suit is the only unbid suit. It is unlikely that the opponents are strong in that suit if they have bid each of the others; otherwise, they probably would have ended up in notrump. The fact that they did not indicates that partner has at least one high honor in the suit.

If your friends keep insisting that you "never lead away from a king," tell them the story about the man who never did. When he passed away he found himself in a bridge game sitting West.

The bidding went

SOUTH	WEST	NORTH	EAST
1 ♡	Pass	3 ♡	Pass
4 ♡	Pass	Pass	Pass

It was his lead with this hand:

♠ K 7 6   ♡ K 3   ◇ K 4 3 2   ♣ K 5 4 3

Then and there he knew where he was!

Another tempting lead for the beginner, besides the singleton, is the ace. The best times to lead aces are against slam bids or when you have only two cards in the suit—in which case you are trying for a ruff.

As a general rule, *if there are two unbid suits and you have the ace in one of them you almost always lead the other*. The reason is that when you lead aces you immediately make the opponents' kings and queens good. If you wait you can often capture a king or queen with your ace. *Aces were not meant to capture deuces and threes*.

Check yourself on the following. Again, you are West and you hear this bidding:

SOUTH	WEST	NORTH	EAST
1 ♠	Pass	2 ♢	Pass
2 ♠	Pass	4 ♠	Pass
Pass	Pass		

It is your lead. In each of these hands, which card do you choose?

(a)	♠ 7 5	♡ K J 7 4	♢ Q 7 6	♣ A 7 6 4
(b)	♠ A 7 6	♡ 8 3	♢ J 10 5 4	♣ A 6 5 4
(c)	♠ Q 9 8 3	♡ Q 8 7 3 2	♢ 6 5	♣ K 2
(d)	♠ 7 6 3	♡ K Q J 5	♢ 6	♣ Q 7 6 5 4
(e)	♠ 3	♡ K 8 7 6 4	♢ 8 6 4	♣ Q 6 5 4
(f)	♠ J 7 6	♡ 6 4	♢ A 6 5 4	♣ A K 8 4
(g)	♠ Q 7 6	♡ 6 4	♢ K Q J 10	♣ J 10 5 4

Solutions

(a) The four of hearts — The choice is between hearts and clubs. Normally, you neither lead the suit that has the ace nor do you consider leading the opponents' suit unless you have a sequence.

(b) The eight of hearts — With A x x of trumps, a short suit lead is very attractive.

(c) The three of hearts — With four trumps, lead your longest side suit.

(d) The king of hearts — Were you able to withstand the temptation of leading the diamond? The strong sequence in hearts is preferred.

(e) The six of hearts — This time your partner probably has four trumps, so you are leading your longest suit for him. Figuring that one out required some real deduction.

(f) The king of clubs — If you are fortunate enough to

have an A K combination, you should lead it.

(g) The king of diamonds   Even though diamonds have been bid, your powerful sequence in the suit makes the lead inviting. As a general rule, avoid leading dummy's first-bid suit. Since declarer usually will attack this suit himself in order to establish the length to obtain discards, you would simply be helping declarer if you led the suit for him.

Finally we come to the trump lead. Should you ever lead a trump, and if so, when? There are two or three times in bridge when a trump lead is mandatory. Here is one of them.

You are West again:

SOUTH	WEST	NORTH	EAST
1 ♠	Dbl.	Pass	Pass
Pass			

This is your hand:

♠ 3   ♡ A J 8 7   ◇ K Q 8 6   ♣ K 9 7 6

You have doubled 1 ♠ to force your partner to bid, yet he has passed! Why? There is only one possible reason that your partner can pass your takeout double—he has good spades; in fact great spades. He must have five or six good spades, and by passing he is saying that he thinks his spades are better than the declarer's. Therefore, you should assist your partner in drawing declarer's trumps. It is as if you were playing the hand in spades: You would try and remove the opposing trumps, wouldn't you?

Well, you should do the same thing here. *Whenever your partner passes a takeout double at the one level he is announcing great strength in trumps, and a trump should be led.*

Now consider this bidding:

SOUTH	WEST	NORTH	EAST
1 ♠	Pass	1 NT	Pass
2 ♡	Pass	Pass	Pass

and your hand (West):

♠ A Q 10 8   ♡ 7 3   ◇ K 7 6 4   ♣ J 8 7

South has bid spades and North has denied good spades by bidding 1 NT. Next, South bids hearts, and North likes hearts better than spades and passes 2 ♡. What do you think North has in spades?

A little thought will tell you that North is very weak in spades, holding perhaps a singleton. South probably has five. What is South going to do with all those spades? Let's look at the hand and we'll see what South is going to do.

DUMMY
♠ 2
♡ 10 5 4
◇ A 9 8 3 2
♣ K 6 5 2

WEST
♠ A Q 10 8
♡ 7 3
◇ K 7 6 4
♣ J 8 7

EAST
♠ 5 4 3
♡ K Q 6 2
◇ Q J 10
♣ Q 10 4

SOUTH
♠ K J 9 7 6
♡ A J 9 8
◇ 6
♣ A 9 3

If you give South a chance (for example, by leading a diamond), South will win the ace, lead the two of spades from the dummy, and finesse the jack. You will win the queen, but subsequently South will lead spades from his hand and trump them in the dummy. Two or three of your good spades will thereby be lost.

In order to prevent South from doing that you lead a trump originally, which immediately removes one trump from the dummy. Now when you get in with the queen of spades you lead a second trump; as it turns out, your partner will win the trick and play a third trump. (On the first trump play partner played the queen forcing the ace.) Now there will be no trumps in the dummy, and South will wind up losing all his spades.

Your trump lead was devastating, because South wanted to use dummy's trumps to trump spades and you knew it. You could tell from the bidding and your own strength in spades what was going to happen.

Whenever declarer bids two suits and you are very strong in the one that does not become trump, a trump lead is usually a good idea.

KEY POINTERS

(1) Your opening lead is the most important card you will play during an entire hand, so give it a little thought. Review the bidding before leading.

(2) As a general rule your first choice should be any suit headed by an A K, in which case you lead the king. Also ranking high on the list of good leads are perfect honor sequences (K Q J, Q J 10, J 10 9) and partner's suit.

(3) If you have an A K combination or a K Q J combination that can be led in preference to partner's suit, do so. In any other case you should lead partner's suit.

(4) Short suit leads are attractive against suit contracts but not when:

  (a) You have natural trump tricks Q J x, K Q J, A J 10, or
  (b) Four trumps.

(5) With four trumps lead your longest suit.
(6) Avoid leading suits that the opponents have bid un-

less you have sequences in those suits. The talk you hear about leading through strength applies mainly to short suit holdings in the dummy

A Q   A Q x   K x x   K J x

almost never through longer, stronger holdings. In that case you will simply be helping declarer develop extra winners.

(7) There is no such rule as "never lead away from a king." Leading away from a king is safer than leading away from either an ace, queen, or jack!

(8) Be careful about laying down aces. Aces are most often led against slam contracts, in suits partner has bid, or when short suited (a singleton or doubleton ace).

(9) If there are two unbid suits and you have the ace in one of the unbid suits you should usually lead the other suit.

(10) A trump lead is marked if partner passes your take-out double at the one level, or if declarer bids two suits, one of which you are strong in and the contract winds up in the other suit.

(11) When leading trumps lead low from two or three small trumps because you may be able to use your bigger ones later. In a side suit you lead top of a doubleton or top of nothing. This does not apply in the trump suit.

(12) The most common lead against suit contracts is the king. It can be from either A K or K Q. If you are in doubt, the dummy and your own hand ought to tell you which it is. (The king might also be led from K x, but this is rare unless partner has bid the suit or desperation has set in.)

(13) From A K all alone lead the ace and then the king. This guarantees a doubleton.

(14) From any king-queen combination lead the king. Against notrump fourth best is led from king-queen combinations that do not have the jack or the ten.

(15) You should remember that the two main ways declarer gets rid of losers are by trumping them in the short hand or discarding them on extra winners. As a defender you must ask yourself which declarer is going to do. If it appears that he is going to trump them in the short hand, then you should lead

trumps. If it appears that he is going to discard them on a strong suit, you should attack the other suits quickly. You can't always tell before the dummy comes down what declarer's intentions will be, but *after* the dummy comes down you should be able to tell and this will guide your subsequent defense.

2

Signaling vs. Suit Contracts

♠ ♡ ◇ ♣

There are three important signals to be learned when defending against suit contracts:
- (1) The high-low,
- (2) The queen from the queen-jack when partner leads the king, and
- (3) The suit-preference return.

THE HIGH-LOW SIGNAL

The first signal we have for use against suit contracts is the high-low signal to show either a doubleton or an equal honor. Partner can usually tell which you mean.

NORTH
♠ Q 6 5
♡ K Q 9 8
◇ A Q J 2
♣ 4 3

WEST
♠ A K 9 8 2
♡ 4 3
◇ 10 9 8
♣ 7 6 5

EAST
♠ 10 3
♡ 5 2
◇ K 7 6 5
♣ Q J 10 9 8

SOUTH
♠ J 7 4
♡ A J 10 7 6
◇ 4 3
♣ A K 2

South plays in 4 ♡ and West leads the king of spades. East

knows immediately that the lead is from ace-king; it can't be from king-queen because the queen is in the dummy.

East also sees that if West will play the ace after the king and then a third round of the suit East can trump. In order to alert West to this possibility East plays the *ten* of spades at trick one. He is beginning a high-low to show either a doubleton or an equal honor.

West, on the other hand, knows that the ten must be the beginning of a high-low to show a *doubleton* because the queen, which is the only equal honor East could have, is in the dummy. (When the king is led against suit contracts the ace and queen are considered equal honors. Against notrump contracts the jack is also considered an equal honor to the king.)

West, therefore, continues with the ace of spades, and when East "completes the echo" by playing the three, West leads a third spade, which East trumps. East exits with the queen of clubs (top of a sequence), and South must eventually take the diamond finesse, which loses. The contract is defeated one trick. Contrast the above hand with this one:

NORTH
♠ Q 6 4
♡ K Q 9 8
◇ A Q 7
♣ 8 5 4

WEST
♠ A K 9 8 2
♡ 4 3
◇ J 10 9 8
♣ 7 6

EAST
♠ 10 7 3
♡ 5 2
◇ K 6 5 2
♣ A J 10 9

SOUTH
♠ J 5
♡ A J 10 7 6
◇ 4 3
♣ K Q 3 2

Once again South plays in 4 ♥ and West leads the king of spades. This time East does not have a doubleton or an equal honor, so he does not begin a high-low. He simply plays the three.

West knows that East does not have a doubleton because East has played his smallest card. West now must realize that laying down the ace is not such a clever play. For one thing, South might trump and dummy's queen would then be good for a discard; or even if South did not trump, the queen would be established for a discard.

In cases like this it is often wise for the defender not to lay down his ace and establish the queen in the dummy. Notice that if West plays a second spade South can later discard his losing diamond on the queen of spades without taking the diamond finesse. South eventually will lose one more trick to the ace of clubs, but he will make his game contract.

Now let's see what happens if West shifts to the jack of diamonds (top of a sequence) before releasing the ace of spades. South would be forced to finesse the queen and East would win the king. The defense would then have two tricks, and they would still make the ace of spades and the ace of clubs to defeat declarer one trick.

One of the hardest—but most necessary—things for a beginning player to remember is that after he leads a king from ace-king he does not always continue with the ace. This is especially true if, as in the hand above, the queen is in the dummy and partner has failed to start a high-low. Only if the defender can see definitely that he will lose his ace if he doesn't take it should he play the ace after the king when the queen is in the dummy and partner has not signaled.

Here is another time it would be unwise to continue with the ace after the king is led:

NORTH
♠ 7 6 5
♡ J 10 9 8
◇ A Q J 9
♣ 4 2

WEST
♠ A K J 3
♡ 7 5 4
◇ 6 3 2
♣ Q J 9

EAST
♠ 9 8 2
♡ 2
◇ 10 8 7 4
♣ A 10 8 7 3

SOUTH
♠ Q 10 4
♡ A K Q 6 3
◇ K 5
♣ K 5 3

South plays in 4 ♡ and West leads the king of spades. East has neither a doubleton nor an equal honor so he plays the two, his lowest spade.

West should realize that South must have the queen of spades and if he leads the ace he will make South's queen good. However, if West can put East on lead in another suit and East returns a spade, West will be able to capture South's queen with the ace; or, if South does not play the queen, West will win the trick with the jack.

West tries to put East in with a club play. (Notice that West does not lead through the strength in diamonds because of the length factor.) West leads the queen of clubs (top of a sequence) and East, knowing from West's lead of the queen that South must have the king, takes the trick with the ace.

East now returns the nine of spades and South is in trouble. If South plays the ten, West will win the jack and then take the ace to set the contract. If South plays the queen, West wins the ace and then takes the jack. In either case South is defeated one trick because West was smart enough *not* to play his ace of spades at trick two.

Here is an example of the "equal honor" high-low:

NORTH
♠ 7 4 3
♡ A Q 5
◊ A K Q J
♣ 8 4 2

WEST
♠ A K 8 5
♡ 4 3 2
◊ 7 6 5
♣ A 6 5

EAST
♠ Q 9 2
♡ 7 6
◊ 10 9 8 4
♣ Q J 10 9

SOUTH
♠ J 10 6
♡ K J 10 9 8
◊ 3 2
♣ K 7 3

This time South settles in a contract of 2 ♡ and West leads his king of spades. East has an equal honor, the queen, and begins his signal (echo) by playing the nine. West realizes that East must have either a doubleton or the queen and in either case it can't hurt to lay down the ace and continue the suit a third time.

East wins the third spade with the queen and would logically shift to the queen of clubs. After taking the first three spade tricks, the defense will then collect the next three club tricks. Once again, accurate defense will defeat the contract one trick.

A few words on the high-low signal: A defender is most apt to give this signal when partner leads the king, which is by far the most common of all leads against suit contracts. There are, however, two times when the high-low is not given with a doubleton:

(1)

DUMMY

♠ 5 4 3

WEST   EAST

♠ K Q 8 7 6   ♠ J 2

DECLARER

♠ A 10 9

Hearts are trump and West leads the king of spades. East cannot be sure whether the lead is from the ace-king or the king-queen. If the lead is from the king-queen, dropping the jack might cost a trick—as it would in this example. Declarer would win the ace and have the ten-nine left in his hand with only the queen to remove.

Therefore, if the queen is not in the dummy, you should not signal your partner high-low with the doubleton jack. If the queen is in the dummy, it is perfectly safe to play the jack because you know your partner has the ace-king:

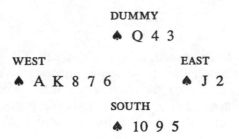

DUMMY

♠ Q 4 3

WEST   EAST

♠ A K 8 7 6   ♠ J 2

SOUTH

♠ 10 9 5

In this case, East should play the jack under the lead of the king to indicate a doubleton.

(2)

DUMMY

♠ 9 7 4

WEST   EAST

♠ K   ♠ Q 6

SOUTH

?

The other occasion that arises when you don't signal with a doubleton is when you have the doubleton queen and your partner leads the king. In this case, play your little one. The play of the queen under the king has a special meaning, which we are about to consider right now.

THE QUEEN FROM THE QUEEN-JACK

When your partner leads the king and you have the queen or the queen-jack, you know that your partner has led from the ace-king. Sometimes it is imperative that your partner know that he can put you on lead immediately. Look at this hand:

NORTH
♠ 7 4
♡ A Q 7 5
◇ A K Q J 10
♣ 3 2

WEST
♠ A K 9 6 3
♡ 3
◇ 6 5 4
♣ A Q 8

EAST
♠ Q J 5 2
♡ 5 2
◇ 9 8 7
♣ J 10 9 7 6

SOUTH
♠ 10 8
♡ K J 10 9 8 4
◇ 3 2
♣ K 5 4

South plays in 4 ♡ and West leads the king of spades. East knows immediately that West has the ace and king, and both defenders should realize when looking at that long, strong diamond suit in dummy that they must take their tricks in the black suits as quickly as possible before declarer throws away his losers on the diamonds.

East plays the *queen* of spades at trick one. This is a specialized signal guaranteeing the jack. In effect, it is equivalent of talking across the table to your partner. It says, "Partner, I know from your lead of the king that you have the ace and king. I have the queen and jack, and it may be important for you to know this. For example, you may want to put me on lead early in the hand. It is entirely safe for you to lead a low spade, as I can take the second trick with my jack."

Now, let's look at the hand from West's point of view after he sees the queen of spades played on the first trick. West has the ace and queen of clubs. It is dangerous to lead the ace when you have the ace-queen because the declarer may have the king and you will be presenting him with a free trick to which he is not entitled.

On the other hand, if your partner leads a club *through* the declarer you must take at least two tricks with your ace and queen of clubs.

Well, you can put your partner on lead if you wish by leading a low spade at trick two to your partner's *guaranteed* jack of spades. When East returns the jack of clubs through South, West must make two club tricks; again, the hand is defeated. If West plays anything other than a low spade at trick two, declarer makes the hand easily.

THE SUIT-PREFERENCE RETURN SIGNAL

Finally we come to a signal used when returning your partner's lead when you think he is going to trump the card you return.

NORTH
♠ Q J 8 7
♡ K Q J
◇ K Q 3
♣ 7 4 2

WEST
♠ 6 4 3
♡ 2
◇ 8 7 4 2
♣ J 10 9 5 3

EAST
♠ 2
♡ A 10 9 7 6 3
◇ A 9 5
♣ Q 8 6

SOUTH
♠ A K 10 9 5
♡ 8 5 4
◇ J 10 6
♣ A K

South lands in 4 ♠ and West leads his singleton two of hearts, hoping his partner has the ace and will return the suit so he can trump. East does have the ace of hearts and can recognize the lead as a singleton. The lead of one's lowest card promises either an honor or a singleton, and since East can see all the lower honor cards in the suit, he knows it is the latter in this case.

Once East recognizes the lead of the deuce as a singleton, he might, in his excitement, return the suit immediately and allow West to trump. West will then have to guess which suit to return in order to trump another heart. In this case, West must return a diamond to East's ace in order to get East in to lead another heart. But what if East had the ace of clubs instead of the ace of diamonds? Then it would be important that West shift to a club at trick three in order to get partner in for another heart lead before declarer pulls the trump.

Obviously, West will not know which suit to return after trumping the heart *unless East tells him*. As you know, talking across the table is strictly forbidden. Conveying information by way of looks and gestures is considered the lowest imaginable form of bridge ethics. Even raising or lowering your voice during the bidding to convey information is illegal. Clearly, we are going to have to tell our partner to return a diamond *by legal means*—with a signal—and we have a signal just for this purpose. It is called the *suit-preference return signal*. Actually, the signal is easier to remember than the name.

It works like this: When your partner leads a short suit or what you have reason to believe is a short suit, you are going to try your hardest to return it as quickly as possible before declarer has a chance to draw partner's trump cards. When you return this suit, you can tell your partner by the size of the card you return which of the remaining two suits (excluding the trump suit) you would like him to return after he trumps.

If you want the higher-ranking suit returned you should return the highest card you can afford in the suit you are leading for your partner to trump. In the example case, the two possible suits for your partner to return are clubs and diamonds, of which diamonds is the higher ranking of the two. So you would return the *ten* of hearts, asking for the diamond shift.

On the other hand, if you wanted a club returned, you would return the three of hearts, the lowest heart you can play, asking your partner to return the lower ranking of the two remaining suits after he trumps your heart lead.

But what if you have no preference which suit your partner returns after he trumps the card you are playing back? In that case, return a neutral middle card, saying, "use your judgment partner. I am not sure which suit I want you to return after you trump this card." Would you like to see this signal in action again?

NORTH
♠ Q 8 3
♡ K 10 2
♢ A K Q 10 7
♣ 5 4

WEST
♠ A K J 9 4
♡ 7 6 3
♢ None
♣ 9 8 7 6 2

EAST
♠ 10 2
♡ 5 4
♢ J 9 8 3 2
♣ Q J 10 3

SOUTH
♠ 7 5 3
♡ A Q J 9 8
♢ 6 5 4
♣ A K

This is a hand that I try on my classes time and again, and they seldom find the winning defense.

South winds up in 4 ♡ and West leads the king of spades. East signals with the ten and West continues with the ace and a third round of spades, which East trumps. East invariably returns the queen of clubs and South takes the rest of the tricks rather easily after drawing trumps.

Had East returned a diamond rather than a club at trick four, West could have trumped and the contract would have been defeated one trick. But how should East know to return a diamond rather than the more normal queen of clubs? *West should tell East which suit to return.* West knows that East is going to trump the third spade, and West, aware of his own void in diamonds, should return the *jack* of spades when giving East a ruff. East should recognize the jack as a rather high card and should return the higher-ranking of the two remaining suits after trumping. If East trusts West he will return a diamond at trick four (providing West returns the jack of spades at trick three), and the contract will be defeated.

Now, if you will remember what you have just read you will be armed with the three most important signals we have against suit contracts. They are:

(1)   The high-low to show either a doubleton or an equal honor. It is used most often when partner leads the king.

(2)   The queen from the queen-jack. This is used exclusively when partner leads the king. It indicates possession of the jack (or perhaps a singleton) and tells the opening leader that it is safe to underlead his ace if he wishes.

(3)   The suit-preference return signal. This is used when giving partner a ruff. If you lead an unnecessarily high card for partner to trump, you are asking partner to return the higher-ranking of the remaining two suits. If you lead a low card for your partner to trump you are asking for the lower-ranking suit to be returned after partner ruffs. If you return a middling card you are telling partner to use his judgment.

Now we are going to test your defense. When defending, you get to see only your hand and the dummy, so that is the case here. You will be told the contract, the bidding and the lead, and you will have to decide what to play.

(1)

DUMMY
♠ A K Q 9 7
♡ J
♢ 10 5
♣ 9 7 6 5 4

WEST
♢ K

EAST (you)
♠ J 10 8
♡ 7 5 2
♢ Q J 6 3
♣ J 10 8

```
        N
    W       E
        S
```

The bidding:

WEST	NORTH	EAST	SOUTH
1 ◊	1 ♠	Pass	4 ♡
Pass	Pass	Pass	

West, your partner, leads the king of diamonds.

(a)   Which diamond do you play? (Don't read further until you have decided.)

(b)   At trick two your partner leads a low diamond (you have played the queen at trick one), and you win the second trick with the jack of diamonds. Which suit do you play now?

(2)

```
          DUMMY
        ♠ A Q J 10
        ♡ A Q 4 3
        ◊ 7 5
        ♣ 7 5 4

 WEST                    EAST (you)
 ♠ 2         N           ♠ K 9 8 7 3
                         ♡ 6 2
             W     E     ◊ J 9 8
                         ♣ A J 10
             S
```

The bidding:

SOUTH	WEST	NORTH	EAST
1 ♡	Pass	3 ♡	Pass
4 ♡	Pass	Pass	Pass

West, your partner leads the deuce of spades. Dummy plays the ten and you win with the king, with declarer playing the four.

(a)   Which suit do you return? Why?

(b)   Which card in that suit do you return? Why?

(3)   DUMMY
             ♠ A J 10 4
             ♡ Q J 6
             ◇ 3 2
             ♣ A Q 4 3

WEST   EAST (you)
♡ K   N   ♠ 3
                         ♡ 9 3
      W   E   ◇ J 10 9 8 5
                         ♣ J 9 8 6 5
             S

The bidding:

NORTH	EAST	SOUTH	WEST
1 ♣	Pass	1 ♠	Dbl.*
2 ♠	Pass	4 ♠	Pass
Pass	Pass		

West leads the king of hearts.

(a)   Which heart do you play? Why?

(b)   Assume that West continues the ace of hearts and then the two of hearts, which you trump. Which suit do you return? Why?

* Takeout double showing an opening bid plus support for the two unbid suits, hearts and diamonds.

(4)   DUMMY
                          ♠ Q 10 2
                          ♡ 7 4 3
                          ◇ 10 5 4
                          ♣ K Q J 10

WEST (you)   EAST
♠ 6 4 3   N   ◇ 2
♡ 9 5 2
◇ A K J 3   W   E
♣ 9 8 2
                          S

The bidding:

SOUTH	WEST	NORTH	EAST
1 ♠	Pass	2 ♠	Pass
4 ♠	Pass	Pass	Pass

This time you lead the king of diamonds. East plays the
deuce.

(a)   Do you continue diamonds at trick two? Why?

(b)   If you do, which card do you play? If you don't,
which suit do you shift to? If you shift, which card do you play
in the suit to which you shift?

(5)   DUMMY
                          ♠ 9 8 5 4
                          ♡ A Q J
                          ◇ K J 10
                          ♣ Q 10 4

WEST (you)   EAST
♠ 7 6   N   ♣ 2
♡ 10 9 8
◇ 7 6 5   W   E
♣ A K J 9 5
                          S

The bidding:

SOUTH	WEST	NORTH	EAST
1 ♠	Pass	2 NT	Pass
3 ♦	Pass	3 ♠	Pass
4 ♠	Pass	Pass	Pass

You lead the king of clubs and partner plays the two.
(a)   Do you continue with clubs?
(b)   If not, to which suit do you shift?

Solutions

(1)   NORTH
          ♠ A K Q 9 7
          ♡ J
          ♦ 10 5
          ♣ 9 7 6 5 4

WEST   EAST
♠ 4 3 2   ♠ J 10 8
♡ 8 6   ♡ 7 5 2
♦ A K 9 8 2   ♦ Q J 6 3
♣ A Q 2   ♣ J 10 8

          SOUTH
          ♠ 6 5
          ♡ A K Q 10 9 4 3
          ♦ 7 4
          ♣ K 3

(a)   Under the king of diamonds you should play the queen to show the jack.
(b)   When partner leads a low diamond to your jack at trick two, you should return a club—specifically, the jack. The spade suit is quite threatening, and you should try to get your club tricks before declarer discards them on his good spades

after drawing trumps. Notice that a club shift by East through declarer's king defeats the contract one trick.

(2)   NORTH
                    ♠ A Q J 10
                    ♡ A Q 4 3
                    ◇ 7 5
                    ♣ 7 5 4

WEST   EAST
♠ 2   ♠ K 9 8 7 3
♡ K 5   ♡ 6 2
◇ 10 6 4 3 2   ◇ J 9 8
♣ Q 9 8 6 3   ♣ A J 10

                    SOUTH
                    ♠ 6 5 4
                    ♡ J 10 9 8 7
                    ◇ A K Q
                    ♣ K 2

(a)   You should return a spade, because your partner's lead of the deuce indicates a singleton or low from an honor. As it can't be low from an honor (you can see all the honors in your hand and dummy), it must be a singleton.

(b)   You know that your partner is going to trump your spade return, so you should return your *three of spades* to ask your partner to come back with a club after trumping the spade. Remember, when you return a low card for your partner to trump he is supposed to return the lower-ranking suit, which in this case is clubs. You will then return another spade, and partner's second ruff will defeat the contract one trick.

(3)

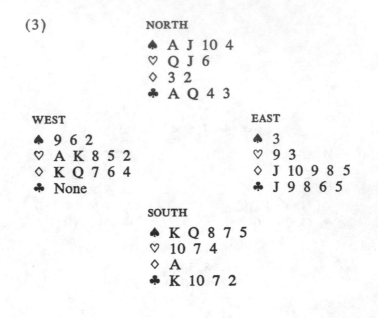

    (a)   You should play the nine of hearts to show a double-ton.

    (b)   You should return a club, because your partner has asked you to. Your partner knew you were going to trump the third round of hearts, so he didn't have to return the deuce. If he wanted you to return a diamond after trumping the heart he would have returned a higher heart.

Bridge is an unusual game. With all the points the opponents have, they cannot make four spades against a good defense; yet your side can make five diamonds with no trouble.

(4)

NORTH
♠ Q 10 2
♡ 7 4 3
◇ 10 5 4
♣ K Q J 10

WEST
♠ 6 4 3
♡ 9 5 2
◇ A K J 3
♣ 9 8 2

EAST
♠ 5 4
♡ A J 10 8 6
◇ 7 6 2
♣ 7 5 4

SOUTH
♠ A K J 9 8
♡ K Q
◇ Q 9 8
♣ A 6 3

(a) You should not continue with diamonds at trick two because your partner's play of the two has denied either a doubleton or the queen. As declarer must have the queen, you must try and put your partner in to lead through the declarer in order to capture the queen.

(b) You should shift to a heart, because the clubs are too strong in the dummy. If your partner has the ace of clubs he will always get in to play a diamond through declarer. But if declarer has the ace of clubs, you must put your partner in immediately in hearts before declarer uses the club suit for discards.

You should shift to the nine of hearts (top of nothing) to tell your partner you have no interest in that suit. East will win the ace and return a diamond, allowing you to take a total of three diamond tricks and one heart to defeat the contract. Had you led the ace of diamonds at trick two you would have made only two diamonds and one heart, and declarer would have made his contract.

(5)   NORTH
                       ♠ 9 8 5 4
                       ♡ A Q J
                       ◇ K J 10
                       ♣ Q 10 4

WEST   EAST
♠ 7 6   ♠ K Q
♡ 10 9 8   ♡ K 6 5 4 3
◇ 7 6 5   ◇ 4 3 2
♣ A K J 9 5   ♣ 7 3 2

                       SOUTH
                       ♠ A J 10 3 2
                       ♡ 7 2
                       ◇ A Q 9 8
                       ♣ 8 6

(a)   You should not continue with clubs. Partner has either three or four small clubs, and either your ace will be trumped or, even if it isn't, you will set up the queen of clubs for a discard.

(b)   Whenever you lead the king, the queen appears in the dummy, and your partner signals you with a low card, you must fear that declarer will later lead up to the queen and use it for a discard. You must always ask yourself in which suit is declarer likely to need one discard?

The bidding on this hand will tell you that declarer has spades and diamonds and is therefore short suited in hearts and clubs. Declarer might use that queen of clubs to discard a losing heart. You should shift to the ten of hearts (top of a sequence) at trick two. Declarer will be forced to finesse the queen, your partner will take the king, and now he will return a club to your ace. In the end your partner will make a trump trick, and you will collect two clubs, one heart, and one spade. Had you impulsively grabbed your ace of clubs at trick two you would have set up the queen for a heart discard, and your partner never would have made a trick with his king of hearts.

KEY POINTERS

(1) Signaling at the bridge table amounts to cheating—legally. You can make the cards speak for you if you use the proper signals and your partner understands them.

(2) The most important signaling comes at trick one, but signals are used by the defense throughout the hand. Without accurate signals defenders are usually in the dark as to what to play. Signals are your seeing-eye dog.

(3) The most important signal at suit contracts is the high-low signal, used most often when partner leads a king, to indicate a doubleton or an equal honor. The equal honor might be either the ace or the queen. The defender who leads the king must watch his partner's card carefully to ascertain whether a high-low is in the making, or a low-high. A low-high signal indicates *no* doubleton or equal honor in the suit being led.

(4) A special signal is used when partner leads the king and you have both the queen and the jack. As partner must have the ace also, you needn't worry about wasting honors. You should play the *queen* to indicate possession of the jack. Frequently partner will be able to play low to your jack and you will be able to lead another suit through declarer that will enable your partner to make an extra trick or two.

(5) When giving partner a ruff you must remember that you can tell him which suit to return after he trumps. This is done by simply leading your lowest card if you want partner to return the lower-ranking suit (outside of trumps) and the highest card you can spare for partner to trump if you want the higher-ranking suit (outside of trumps) returned. Assume for a moment that diamonds are trump and you are leading a heart, which you know your partner is going to trump. If you want your partner to return a club (the lower-ranking suit), you should return a low heart for him to ruff; if you want a spade back (the higher-ranking suit), you should return a high heart.

(6) In addition to these signals, the defenders also use many of the signals that were discussed in Signaling vs. Notrump.

(a) The count signal is used against suit contracts. Whenever declarer attempts to establish his long suit in dummy, the defender with weakness in that suit is supposed to play high-low with a doubleton or low-high with three cards.

(b) The discard signal is also used against suit contracts. When you are discarding (perhaps on the trump suit), a high discard in a suit indicates strength in that suit, and a low discard indicates weakness. If one can make two discards in the same suit, a high-low discard (perhaps the seven followed by the three) indicates strength in the suit, but a low-high discard (perhaps the seven followed by the eight) indicates weakness.

(7) As a general rule for signaling you should remember this: If your partner leads an honor card to a trick and you like the suit he has led, encourage your partner to continue the suit by giving him as high a spot-card as you can afford. If, on the other hand, you wish him to play something else play a low card.

(8) No doubt you are beginning to think that there are too many signals for you to remember. Don't worry about remembering all the signals at once; it's almost impossible unless you play quite a bit. Most players confuse signaling with leading. When you *lead* a low card, you are promising strength in the suit.

Maybe this chart will help:

Leading a low card indicates strength.
Discarding a low card indicates weakness.
Leading a high spot-card indicates weakness.
Discarding a high spot-card indicates strength.

3

Second-Hand Play

♠ ♡ ◇ ♣

You have just arrived at the turning point of your defensive career! If you can understand "second-hand play," in one fell swoop you will have passed up ninety percent of the world's bridge players.

Why is second-hand play so difficult? Mainly because you have to think. However, don't worry. There are a few rules that will eliminate most of your problems—but not all.

For a start, you must keep in mind that when you are second to play either the dummy or the declarer will be the first. When dummy leads a suit first we have this situation:

DUMMY

WEST   EAST (you)

DECLARER

In this situation, you are second to play and you cannot see the hand that plays after you.

Alternately you may be sitting in the West position:

DUMMY

WEST (you)   EAST

DECLARER

In this case, declarer leads the suit first and you can see the hand that plays after you. It goes without saying that it is easier to know what to play in this circumstance.

In all the following examples you are to assume that South is the declarer and the contract is notrump. Second-hand play varies slightly between notrump and suit contracts, but any variance will be mentioned.

Finally, an excellent move to make before attacking this chapter is to remove the spade suit from any nearby deck of cards. Lay out all the diagram positions in front of you and follow the explanations card for card. The extra time required to do this will be refunded a hundredfold when you are actually at the bridge table.

DUMMY IS TO YOUR RIGHT

You will begin by assuming that the dummy is to your right and that declarer is leading from dummy. You are East, second to play. For purposes of simplicity the suit will always be spades.

DUMMY

♠ Q 9 2

WEST   EAST (you)

♠ K 10 6

SOUTH

?

Assume that the dummy leads the deuce and you are next to play. Which card should you play—the six, ten, or king?

Rather than be tormented every time this type of situation comes up you should remember the general rule:

When dummy is to your right and declarer leads a low card from dummy, second hand should also play a low card. Therefore, the correct play with the East hand is the six. Perhaps you have heard the expression, "second hand low." It is to this type of play that the expression refers.

However, if dummy leads the queen, East should cover with the king. *When an honor is led from dummy, second hand covers*

an honor with a higher honor if he has one. You will remember
that the ten-spot or higher is considered an honor.

Simply remembering these two rules (*second hand low* and
cover an honor with an honor) will allow you to survive in most
bridge games until you learn when these rules don't apply. There
is no bridge rule without an exception.

It might be added here that most players follow these two
rules without ever knowing why. However, once you know why,
your second-hand play will become a little more polished.

All right. Why does second hand play low when a low card
is led from dummy? Study this example closely:

DUMMY

♠ Q 9 2

WEST   EAST (you)

♠ J 8 7 3   ♠ K 10 6

SOUTH

♠ A 5 4

Dummy leads the two and you are second to play. Remember, *you cannot see the declarer's hand.* First, notice what happens if you play your king. Declarer, who was going to play the
ace anyway, now captures your king, which automatically makes
the queen in dummy high.

Next let's see what happens if you play your ten. Declarer
wins the ace and might decide to lead a little one back and
finesse the nine. This will force your king and again make
dummy's queen good—two tricks for declarer.

Now let's do it right. You play your six and declarer wins
the ace. You still have the K 10 hovering over dummy's Q 9,
and declarer takes only one trick, the ace.

A typical statement at this point is: Fine, I can see that I
should not play my king if declarer has the ace, but how do I
know that? What if my partner has the ace?

All right. We are going to give your partner the ace and see
what happens:

DUMMY

♠ Q 9 2

WEST   EAST (you)

♠ A 8 7 3   ♠ K 10 6

SOUTH

♠ J 5 4

Dummy leads the deuce. If you play the king, it takes the trick. Your partner takes a second trick with the ace, but the opponents still make one trick with the queen.

However, if you play the six, declarer will play the jack and your partner will win the ace. Now you will retain the king-ten over dummy's queen and you will take three tricks to declarer's none.

You can see that even if your partner has the ace it still pays to play low. *Honor cards should be used either to capture or to cover other honor cards.*

Another important point is that when dummy leads a low card you normally play low and do not play a middle card, such as a nine or ten, to signal your partner that you are strong in the suit. Nines and tens are too important to squander. Very often you will be throwing away a trick. For the time being, either play your lowest card or cover an honor with an honor.

To return to the second rule, why cover? The average beginning player sees covering as simply wasting an honor. When a queen is led from dummy the beginner hesitates to cover for fear that the king will be lost to the ace.

This is the type of thinking that you must eliminate immediately! Look:

DUMMY

♠ Q 3

WEST   EAST (you)

♠ 9 8 7 5 2   ♠ K 10 6

SOUTH

♠ A J 4

If dummy leads the queen and East covers (correctly), South wins the ace. South also wins the jack, *but East wins the third trick with the ten.*

Now let's see what happens if East plays the six (incorrectly) under the queen. Declarer plays the four and the queen takes the trick. Dummy now leads the deuce and South remains with the A J over East's K 10. South simply covers the ten with the jack and takes all three tricks. In this case, covering the queen with the king will *promote* the ten to a third-round winner for you. This is the reason for covering in the first place: *To promote lower cards (tens and nines) for either you or your partner.*

The foregoing statement should also answer your next question, "But what if I didn't have the ten?"

The answer is that you are covering in hopes your partner has the ten.

                              DUMMY
                              ♠ Q 3

        WEST   EAST (you)
        ♠ 10 8 7   ♠ K 5 4

                              SOUTH
                              ♠ A J 9 6 2

If you cover the queen with the king your partner will eventually make a trick with the ten. If you do not cover, declarer will take five tricks instead of four. (Declarer will play low on the queen and then finesse the jack.)

If your partner does not have the ten it doesn't matter whether you cover or not because your king will never take a trick anyway. You might as well cover.

DUMMY

♠ Q 3 2

WEST   EAST (you)

♠ 8 7 6   ♠ K 5 4

SOUTH

♠ A J 10 9

Dummy leads the queen. If you cover, South takes the king with his ace and the jack, ten, and nine are all good. However, if you don't cover, the queen takes the trick. Then a low card is led to declarer's ten, the ace catches your king, and you still don't take a trick.

The whole point is to show you that you are not wasting your honor when it is used to cover another honor. Let your kings die valiantly! Remember that your kings won't rebel if you use them to smother queens! They will even be proud to come to rest on jacks and tens. For that matter queens also like to smother jacks and tens.

DUMMY

♠ J 5

WEST   EAST

♠ 9 4 3 2   ♠ Q 7 6

SOUTH

♠ A K 10 8

Assume that you are East and the jack is led from dummy. You should cover with the queen, but watch what happens. Declarer takes your queen with the king or ace. His ten is also high, but in the end your partner takes a trick with the nine! Had you not covered the jack it would have taken the trick, your queen would have fallen under the ace, and declarer would make all four tricks instead of the three to which he is entitled.

Don't be stingy if an honor is led from dummy.

Now that you are sold on covering an honor with an honor you must be told that there is one huge exception!

When dummy has two or more equal honors, second hand should cover the last equal honor that is led.

DUMMY

♠ Q J 9

WEST   EAST (you)

♠ 10 8 7 6   ♠ K 3 2

SOUTH

♠ A 5 4

If dummy leads the queen or jack, you must cover not the first honor but the second one. Why? Observe what happens if you cover the queen. South will take your king and can, if he wishes, play a small spade and finesse dummy's nine, giving South all three tricks in the suit.

Now let's see what happens if you cover the second (or last) equal honor. The queen is led and ducked all around. Next the jack is led, which you cover. Declarer wins the ace, but your partner's ten stands up for a third-round trick.

If declarer had had the ten, it wouldn't have mattered which honor you covered as you would have been unable to take a trick in any case. However, proper technique is to *cover the last equal honor being led from dummy*.

For purposes of a quiz, assume that you are East:

(1)   DUMMY

♠ J 10 3

EAST (you)

♠ Q 7 6

(a) If dummy leads the jack first which card do you play?

(b) If dummy leads the ten first which card do you play?

(c) If dummy leads the three, which card do you play?

(2)   DUMMY

♠ Q 8 3

EAST (you)

♠ K 9 2

(a)   If dummy leads the queen, which card do you play?

(b)   If dummy leads the eight, which card do you play?

(c)   If dummy leads the three, which card do you play?

Solutions

(1a)	Play the six.	Prepare to cover the last equal honor.
(1b)	Play the six.	Same reason as above.
(1c)	Play the six.	When dummy plays a low card, you play a low card.
(2a)	Play the king.	Cover an honor with an honor unless there is an equal honor in dummy.
(2b)	Play the two.	As a general rule, spot-cards are not covered.
(2c)	Play the two.	When dummy plays a low card, you play a low card.

In none of the examples given did second hand have the ace. What should second hand do with the ace—take the trick, or play low?

At this point the reader is gently reminded that any "rule" dealing with either the bidding, play, or defense is simply a guide. Each hand is different, and for that reason one is always developing at the game of bridge.

Until now, our general rule for second-hand play has been to play low if dummy plays low and to cover an honor with an honor unless there are two or more equal honors in dummy.

Note that when you have the ace of the suit being led (remember, this is notrump), you cannot lose it if you play low. You will simply make it later. In a suit contract the situation is not always as clear, and even the best players have been known to err.

However, as a general rule, *do not play your ace the first time the suit is led unless it happens to be the setting trick or you can use it to cover another honor.* Naturally there are exceptions to this. One notable one is at notrump when you are anxious to return your partner's original lead. In this case you might play the ace in order to do so.

Even though it is generally right to play low the first time the suit in which you have the ace is led, the beginning player has trouble understanding why. This deal will help explain:

NORTH
♠ A Q 10 2
♡ 5 4 3 2
◇ A K Q
♣ A 2

WEST
♠ 4
♡ Q 10 8 7
◇ 4 3 2
♣ Q J 10 9 8

EAST
♠ 6 5
♡ A 9 6
◇ 8 7 6 5
♣ 7 6 5 4

SOUTH
♠ K J 9 8 7 3
♡ K J
◇ J 10 9
♣ K 3

South plays in a contract of 6 ♠, and West leads the queen of clubs. Looked at from South's point of view, this hand has losers in exactly one suit—hearts.

Sooner or later South must lead a heart from dummy (weakness to strength). If East panics and flies up with the ace, South will be quite pleased. South will play the jack under the ace, the king will be good, and he will make his slam easily.

But what if East casually plays the six when dummy leads a low heart? Unless East is sitting too close to the table, South will not know who has the ace of hearts. He may decide West has it and insert the jack hoping to drive out the ace—a reasonable play, but not on this hand. West would win the queen, and the next time hearts is played East would fly up with the ace because it would then be the *setting trick*. Also, if the contract had been seven spades or seven notrump, East would fly up with the ace of hearts the first time the suit was led because, again, it would constitute the *setting trick*.

Now you know the reason for ducking with an ace the first time the suit is led. You force declarer to guess in case he has both the king and the jack.

Still another reason for ducking with an ace can be seen by studying this layout:

DUMMY

♠ Q 3 2

WEST   EAST (you)

♠ 10 7 6 4   ♠ A J 5

SOUTH

♠ K 9 8

Assume dummy leads the two. If you play the ace, declarer makes two tricks, the king and the queen. If you play low, declarer will win the king but later you will make both your ace and jack and declarer will be held to only one trick. In other words, your ace shouldn't capture thin air. By holding it back one time you will be able to capture dummy's queen later in the play. Notice also that it would be a serious error to play the jack the first time. Declarer would win the king and then could finesse the nine and drive out your ace.

The idea of giving declarer problems (or puzzles) arises in a somewhat similar situation:

DUMMY

♠ A 3 2

WEST   EAST (you)

♠ J 9 8 7   ♠ K 5 4

SOUTH

♠ Q 10 6

Assume that North leads a low card from dummy and you, East, are second to play. You can see the ace in dummy, so you know your king will take the trick; but should you play the king?

This is a most difficult question to answer. Suffice it to say that half the time it is right to duck and half the time it is right to win the king! This is one of the aspects that makes bridge a challenging game.

In the diagram situation it would be better for East to play low. South does not know who has the king (unless East has given away the show by thinking about what to play) and will almost always finesse the ten, hoping to drive out the king. In this case, the ten would drive out the jack and you would make your king later.

Again, if the king were the *setting trick* you would play it at your earliest opportunity.

Now we move into a different area. If second hand has two or three equal honor cards and wants to insure a trick, which honor should be played?

DUMMY

♠ 4 3 2

WEST   EAST (you)

♠ 9 7 6   ♠ K Q J 8

SOUTH

♠ A 10 5

Dummy leads a low card. East is naturally afraid to play the eight for fear declarer might win a trick with the ten. East can assure himself at least two tricks in the suit by simply playing one of his equal honors. Whenever a defensive player decides to play from equal honors he should play his *lower* or *lowest* equal.

When playing from equals it is easiest to remember that you play the same honor on defense that you would if your partner had led the suit to you. For example, in the diagram situation, if *West* leads the nine and dummy plays low, East should play the jack. Similarly, if dummy leads the suit first East should again play the jack. Only if *East* leads the suit originally should the king be led. (*Lead top of a sequence but follow suit with the bottom of the sequence.*)

Again, as a general rule, a defender should tend to play one of his equal honors when he has *three* or *more* equal honors and not to play an honor at all with only two equal honors. Which card should East play in the following situations?

NORTH (dummy)

♠ 4 3 2

EAST (you)

(a) ♠ J 10 6
(b) ♠ J 10 9 7
(c) ♠ Q J 6
(d) ♠ Q J 10 7
(e) ♠ K Q 6
(f) ♠ K Q J 8 5
(g) ♠ A K 5

Solutions

(a)   You should play the six because you have only two equal honors. However, it should be stated that there are times (usually later in the hand) when you will wish to play one of your two equals. If this is the case you should play your ten (lower equal).

(b) With three equal cards a defender should play his lowest equal. The nine is the correct card.

(c) The six is correct with only two equals. However, later in the hand you might decide to play your jack (if for example, the ace has already been played and you wish to insure yourself one trick).

(d) The ten is the correct card here—lowest of equals.

(e) This presents a choice. If you wish to gamble for two tricks you can play low. If you want a quick trick you should play your queen, which will force out the ace and promote your king. At notrump you usually play low the first time in this situation, but defending against a suit contract you usually play your queen.

(f) The jack—lowest of equals.

(g) The king, *even though you have only two equals. It would be a little far out to play low in this case unless you felt you absolutely needed three tricks in the suit.*

You have just covered the most difficult aspect of second-hand play—when declarer plays *after you and you cannot see his hand.*

DUMMY IS TO YOUR LEFT

Just think how much clearer the situation becomes when you can see the cards in the hand that plays after you. That is precisely the situation when dummy is to your *left* and declarer leads up to dummy. In this case you are West.

Notice the difference in this simple example:

DUMMY

♠ A

WEST (you)   EAST

♠ K Q J 4   ♠ 5 3

SOUTH

♠ 10 9 8 7 6 2

Assume that South leads a small spade up to dummy's ace. If you couldn't see the lone ace you would play your jack (lowest of three equals), to make sure you make at least two tricks. But in this case you needn't waste your jack because you can see that the ace is going to be played anyway. You eventually take three tricks instead of two.

Now consider this familiar situation:

DUMMY

♠ K J 10

WEST (you)   EAST

♠ A 8 7 6   ♠ Q 5 4 3

SOUTH

♠ 9 2

Assume South leads a low spade towards dummy and you can see the K J 10. What should you do? That's an easy one. Any time you can see two or three honors in the dummy with a "hole" (divided strength such as K J 10, Q 10 8, A J 9, A 10 7 4, as opposed to solid strength such as Q J 10 or K Q J you should unhesitatingly play *low*, even if you have a card that can take the trick.

Declarer is very apt to insert a lower honor such as the nine, ten, or jack, which your partner might be able to win. The next time the suit is led you can take your ace. This idea of ducking even though you can take the trick is very important, and unless the trick you can take is the setting one don't panic. Simply play low; it will usually result in the gain of a trick!

Study this diagram:

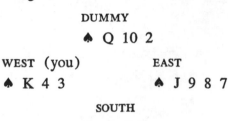

DUMMY

♠ Q 10 2

WEST (you)   EAST

♠ K 4 3   ♠ J 9 8 7

SOUTH

♠ A 6 5

Assume that South leads the five towards the dummy. You in the West position should play low without a pause—and not as if you were praying. Remember, you don't want to give away the fact that you could have taken the trick. Declarer with divided strength in dummy (a hole) is very apt to be taken in by your nonchalance. He will probably figure East for the king, as you made no effort to take the trick. With this in mind, South will usually insert the ten—hoping to drive out the king But you will have fooled South. Your partner has the jack and not the king. He will win the jack and you will take your king later. Even if declarer guesses correctly and plays the queen when you play low, most of the time you will still make your king later in the hand.

Here is another common situation:

DUMMY

♠ K 5 4

WEST (you)　　　　　　EAST

♠ A 7 6　　　　　　♠ J 10 9 8

SOUTH

♠ Q 3 2

South leads the deuce toward the dummy. This time declarer has no choice. There is no hole in the dummy, but you should still play low and allow the king to take the trick. If you run up with your ace, the king will still be a good trick, but, worse, you will have established the queen in declarer's hand for a second trick.

If you play low and allow the king to win, you will then be in a position to capture declarer's queen with your ace, and declarer will make one trick instead of two.

By now you should see that when declarer leads up to an honor or an honor combination in dummy it usually pays to play low the first time even if you can take the trick unless, of course, it is the setting trick, in which case you should not take any unnecessary risks.

One of the most serious errors that the beginning player can make when he plays before dummy is to "force honors out of the dummy." For example:

DUMMY

♠ A 9 6 5

WEST (you)   EAST
♠ K 10 2   ♠ Q

SOUTH

♠ J 8 7 4 3

Assume that South leads a low card up to the dummy. *When dummy has higher cards than you, simply play low.* In other words, do not play the ten to "force" the ace out of the dummy. Ninety-nine times out of a hundred the ace will be played anyway, and your ten might be a vital card. In this case it would be a trick.

Situations like this also cause the beginning player frustration:

DUMMY

♠ A Q J

WEST (you)   EAST
♠ K 4 3   ♠ 10 9 8 6

SOUTH

♠ 7 5 2

South leads a low card up to dummy, and you can see the A Q J. Do not, under any circumstances, play the king! Your only chance to take a trick with the king is to play low. Who knows what declarer is going to do! He may play the ace, making your king good. Even if declarer finesses the queen, you are better off than if you had played your king. You might yet take a trick with it.

A defender simply must accept the inevitability of not being able to take tricks with honor cards if higher honor cards are sitting behind him. The only possible chance to come to a trick in cases like this to to play *low*.

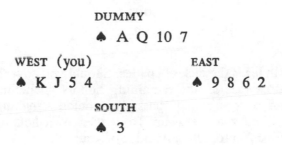

DUMMY

♠ A Q 10 7

WEST (you)   EAST

♠ K J 5 4   ♠ 9 8 6 2

SOUTH

♠ 3

South leads a low spade. You should see at a glance that it will do you no good to play an honor because dummy will simply top it with a higher honor. Play low and hope for the best. Declarer may play the ace.

Should second hand ever play high? Of course. Second hand may wish to split (play one of his equal honors), or he may wish to cover an honor with an honor.

Remember, we haven't discussed the situations in which declarer is leading an honor from the closed hand towards the dummy. In all these examples declarer has been leading a small card up to dummy's honor strength.

TO COVER OR NOT TO COVER

We said earlier that when an honor card was led from the *dummy,* second hand generally covered an honor with an honor in the hopes of *promoting a lower honor for either himself or his partner.* Do you remember when you covered an honor led from the dummy and you couldn't see what the declarer held you had to *hope* that you were promoting something for your partner or for yourself?

Now you can see the dummy and you can decide whether there is any possible chance for promotion:

DUMMY
♠ A Q 10 9

WEST (you)   EAST
♠ K 7 6 2   ?

SOUTH
?

South leads the jack of spades. Should you cover? Of course not! You can see *all* the remaining honors, including the nine, in dummy so you cannot possibly promote anything for your partner. (And you are aware from your own holding that you cannot possibly promote anything for yourself.)

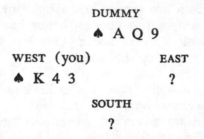

DUMMY
♠ A Q 9

WEST (you)   EAST
♠ K 4 3   ?

SOUTH
?

Once again, South leads the jack of spades. Should you cover? This time you should. If you cover and partner has the ten of spades, it will become a third-round winner. If declarer has the ten of spades, you cannot get a trick whether you cover or not.

DUMMY
♠ A J 10 2

WEST (you)   EAST
♠ K 9 8 7   ?

SOUTH
?

South leads the queen of spades. Do you cover? You should. If you cover you will take a fourth-round trick in the suit with your nine. If you don't and declarer has three spades, you won't take any tricks. Study the entire diagram:

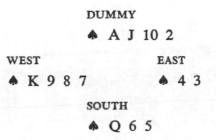

DUMMY

♠ A J 10 2

WEST   EAST

♠ K 9 8 7   ♠ 4 3

SOUTH

♠ Q 6 5

If you duck the queen, it will take the trick, with dummy playing the deuce. South will continue with a small card and the best you can do is play low; the ten will be successfully finessed. South, if he can, will then come back to his hand in a different suit and lead his remaining small card, finessing dummy's jack, and you will not take a single spade trick.

If the dummy held not the deuce of spades, but simply A J 10, then it would have been quite correct *not* to cover. *When there are four cards in dummy the nine is often a vital card.* Now try this one:

DUMMY

♠ A K 10 2

WEST (you)   EAST

♠ Q 5 4   ?

SOUTH

?

South leads the jack. Do you cover? Your answer is yes. You should hope that your partner has the nine with three other small cards. In that case, the nine will become a fourth-round trick.

Another tip when deciding whether to cover or not: Ask yourself what the dummy will look like if you don't cover and declarer finesses the honor that he is leading: Back to our previous example:

DUMMY

♠ A K 10 2

WEST (you)   EAST

♠ Q 5 4   ♠ 9 8 6 3

SOUTH

♠ J 7

As you recall, South led the jack. Sitting West, you should picture what the dummy will look like if you play low and dummy also plays low. The dummy will remain with the ace-king-ten. Your queen is sure to fall under the ace and king, and the ten will then be good. This means that declarer will take four tricks in the suit if you do not cover.

Now picture the dummy if you do cover. The ace-ten-deuce will remain in dummy, and if your partner also started with four cards in the suit declarer will be held to three tricks.

Now try this one:

DUMMY

♠ A 2

WEST (you)   EAST

♠ K 4 3   ?

SOUTH

?

South leads the queen. Should you cover? It would be unwise. Notice that this time the dummy has a doubleton ace. If you play low and allow the queen to win, the ace will take the next trick but you will take the third trick with your king.

You must assume when South leads the queen and the jack is not in the dummy that he has the jack. It would be a bad play on the declarer's part to lead a queen without the jack to back it up, and we must assume that declarer knows what he is doing. By playing low you have saved a trick, because this was the situation:

DUMMY

♣ A 2

WEST   EAST

♠ K 4 3   ♠ 9 8 7 6 5

SOUTH

♠ Q J 10

Had you covered, South would have taken three tricks. By playing low, you hold him to two.

Consider this situation, which is very typical:

NORTH

♠ A 4 3

WEST   EAST

♠ Q 6 5   ♠ 7 2

SOUTH

♠ K J 10 9 8

South leads the jack, trying to coax West to cover. If West is smart he will play low, because he will know that South has the ten and there is no point in covering. South might think that East has the queen, play the ace, and finesse right into West. So West will actually take a trick with the queen in this situation nine times out of ten if he doesn't cover—providing no anxiety is obvious before he makes up his mind. A second cousin to the above diagram is this run-of-the-mill position that finds defenders losing hundreds of tricks during the course of their bridge careers:

DUMMY

♠ A 4 3

WEST   EAST

♠ Q 6 5   ♠ K 9 8 7

SOUTH

♠ J 10 2

South leads the jack, and West makes the foolish play of covering with the queen. This allows dummy to take the ace and later lead low towards the jack. East wins the king, but South makes the jack for a total of two tricks.

If West plays low when the jack is led, East will win the king and South will be held to one trick in the suit. (If South leads the ten the second time, West will cover.)

We finally must conclude that: *If declarer leads a queen or a jack from the closed hand and the immediate lower honor is not visible, declarer has that lower honor and you should not cover the first honor.*

Don't let this throw you. In order to understand the above rule all you have to do is turn yourself around and pretend you are East and can see the dummy:

DUMMY

♠ Q J 9

WEST   EAST (you)

♠ 10 8 7 6   ♠ K 5 4

SOUTH

♠ A 3 2

Remember we said that if the queen was from dummy, you should not cover the first equal honor but the last. In this case, that means you should duck the queen but cover the jack.

If you do this properly, partner will make a trick with the

ten. If you cover the first honor, declarer will be able to finesse the nine and take three tricks.

Now turn yourself back around again and assume the West position:

DUMMY

♠ A 4 3

WEST (you)   EAST

♠ K 5 4   ♠ 10 8 7 6

SOUTH

♠ Q J 9

South leads the queen. What should you do? You should duck, on the assumption that South has the jack, and cover not the first equal honor but the last. Assume the jack is led next. You are not sure who has the ten but you must cover in hopes it it your partner. If you could see that declarer had Q J 10, you would not cover the jack either; but you can't, so you must hope partner has it.

What if the honor beneath the one that declarer is leading is visible in either your own hand or the dummy?

If the honor is in your hand you should cover:

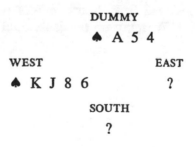

DUMMY

♠ A 5 4

WEST   EAST

♠ K J 8 6   ?

SOUTH

?

South leads the queen. You can see that if you cover you immediately promote your jack; that is reason enough.

When the next-lower honor is visible in dummy things are not always as clear:

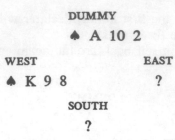

DUMMY

♠ A 10 2

WEST   EAST

♠ K 9 8   ?

SOUTH

?

South leads the jack. Should West cover? The rule is that if the lower honor is visible in the dummy you should cover if there is any chance at all for promotion. In this case there is a good chance for promotion, as your partner might have the queen. This could easily be the position:

DUMMY

♠ A 10 2

WEST   EAST

♠ K 9 8   ♠ Q 7 6 5 4

SOUTH

♠ J 3

If West ducks the jack, South makes two tricks by later finessing the ten. If West covers the jack, South makes only one trick.

Now try this one:

DUMMY

♠ A 10 9 8 7 6

WEST   EAST

♠ Q 5 4   ?

SOUTH

?

South leads the jack. Should West cover? Only if he wants to lose his present partner for life. Even though the immediate lower honor is in dummy there isn't a ghost of a chance for promotion, and partner's king might be a singleton. Wouldn't you feel silly if you played the queen, dummy played the ace, and partner the king?

COVERING HONORS IN THE TRUMP SUIT

This is a very delicate subject, and no matter how expert you are you are bound to make some unfortunate decisions. (That's the term experts use when they make a mistake.)

When it comes to making a decision about covering an honor with an honor in the trump suit, the important point is to have some idea as to declarer's length in the suit. This comes from listening to the bidding. For example:

DUMMY

♠ J 3

WEST   EAST (you)

?   ♠ Q 5 4

SOUTH

?

Spades are trump and dummy leads the jack. Should you cover? Before we can answer that question intelligently we must consider the bidding. Assume that South has opened with 3 ♠.

We know that an opening bid of 3 ♠ shows a seven-card suit (once in a while a six-card suit). So your partner figures to have one spade. If you remember that the only reason you cover an honor with an honor in the first place is to promote something for either yourself or your partner, in this case it would be clearly wrong to cover as you could not promote anything for yourself and you know your partner has a singleton. It would be foolish to cover. The suit may have been divided originally:

DUMMY

♠ J 3

WEST   EAST

♠ 6   ♠ Q 5 4

SOUTH

♠ A K 10 9 8 7 2

South probably has no intention of finessing the jack of spades holding nine spades between the two hands. He is simply trying to bait you into covering. But you're too smart. You play low "smoothly," as if you hadn't a care in the world. South will think that you don't have the queen and will play the ace and the king and your queen will stand up.

Now let's say the bidding has gone like this:

SOUTH	NORTH
1 ♣	1 ◊
1 ♠	Pass

and the spade situation is somewhat similar, namely:

DUMMY

♠ J 3 2

                    EAST (you)

                    ♠ Q 5 4

Once again the jack is led from dummy. Should you cover? This time you should. South is playing the hand in his second suit, which is typically a four-card suit. If South has four spades, partner has three, and one of them might be the ten. Or he might even have better spades. It may look like this:

DUMMY

♠ J 3 2

WEST   EAST (you)

♠ A 9 6   ♠ Q 5 4

SOUTH

♠ K 10 8 7

If you cover the jack with the queen, South will play the king and partner will win the ace. South's ten will be the highest trump, but partner's nine will take the third trick in trumps. All in all, by covering you will manage to take two trump tricks.

If you don't cover, the jack will force the ace, and the next time declarer will lead low from dummy and finesse the ten. Your queen will fall under the king and declarer will lose only one trick instead of two.

Therefore, before covering an honor in the trump suit you must consider partner's probable length in the trump suit. If he has a singleton you should realize that you are not promoting anything for him if you cover; so if you are not promoting anything for yourself, don't cover.

Extending this principle a step further we find that often we must be careful about covering an honor with an honor at notrump if declarer has shown considerable length in the suit during the bidding. Consider this bidding:

SOUTH	NORTH
1 ♣	1 ♠
3 ♣	3 ♡
3 NT	Pass

Let's assume that as East your club suit is:

DUMMY

♣ Q 5 4 3

WEST   EAST (you)

?   ♣ K 2

SOUTH

?

South has shown a six- or seven-card suit by jumping in the suit. If dummy should lead the queen of clubs it would be folly to cover. West has at most a singleton club and may even be void. If partner is void, declarer has seven clubs. With eleven clubs between the two hands declarer may not even be intending to finesse! *With this bidding,* a casual two would be the best play.

On the other hand, if you cannot be sure of the club length in the declarer's hand (the bidding may not have been so revealing), you should cover the queen in hopes of promoting a possible ten in your partner's hand.

Now let's see how much you have digested. First, there is a quiz to see how you handle yourself when you are East and can't see the hand that plays after you (the closed hand). Then you move to West where dummy, or the exposed hand, plays after you. All the pertinent information, such as the bidding, whether you are defending a trump contract or notrump, and so forth, will be given.

Part I

You are East and cannot see the hand that plays after you.
(1)   Declarer is leading a suit at notrump and you have no indication as to his length in the suit.

DUMMY

♠ J 10 4

WEST   EAST (you)

?   ♠ K 7 5

SOUTH

?

(a)   If dummy leads the jack, which card would you play?
(b)   If dummy leads the ten, which card would you play?
(c)   If dummy leads the four, which card would you play?

(2)   It is again notrump, and there is no indication as to declarer's length. South leads a low card from dummy. Which card would you play with each of the following holdings?

DUMMY

♠ 7 4 3

WEST   EAST (you)

?   (a) K 9 6 2
                        (b) Q J 10
                        (c) A 8 5
                        (d) J 10 9 8 2
                        (e) Q J 5 2

SOUTH

?

(3)   This time, you are dealing with the trump suit. You know from the bidding that declarer has either a five- or a six-card suit in the closed hand behind you. South leads the jack from the dummy. Which card would you play with each of the following holdings?

       DUMMY

       ♠ J 4 3

  WEST   EAST (you)

   ?   (a) K 10 9

           (b) Q 7 6 5

           (c) A 5 2

           (d) K 5

           (e) K 6 5 2

     SOUTH

      ?

Solutions

Part I

(1a)	The five	Cover the last of equal honors.
(1b)	The five	Cover the last of equal honors.
(1c)	The five	When dummy starts with a low card you generally play low also.
(2a)	The two	Unless second hand has a specific reason for playing an honor he should normally play low when dummy leads a low card towards the closed hand.
(2b)	The ten	The lowest of equal honors, just as if partner had led the suit to you.
(2c)	The five	Unless the ace would be the setting trick.
(2d)	The eight	Lowest of equals.
(2e)	The two	Normally a defender must have three equals to put one up in this situation (the main exception being the ace and the king).
(3a)	The king	You are promoting the ten as a third-round trick for yourself.
(3b)	The five	Partner has at most a singleton, so you cannot promote anything for him by covering. Your own spot-cards are so small

that you cannot promote anything for yourself by covering, so you should play low.
Partner might even have the singleton
king.

(3c)   The two   Perhaps declarer is going to finesse the jack
and your partner will win the queen. (In a
side suit an ace sometimes covers a jack,
but not in the trump suit when partner is
known to be short.)

(3d)   The king   Partner has two or three cards in the suit,
and if one of them is the ten there is a
good chance for promotion.

(3e)   The two   Same reason as (3b).

Part II

You are West and dummy is the hand that plays after you.

(1)   Declarer is leading up to dummy at a notrump contract. He is evidently trying to establish this suit. In each case,
declarer leads the six. Which card would you play?

DUMMY

♠ K J 9 3

WEST (you)   EAST

(a) A 10 8 7   ?
(b) Q 5
(c) A 4 2

SOUTH

Leads six

(2)   Same situation as in (1). Declarer leads the six up
to dummy at notrump. Which card would you play in each case?

DUMMY

♠ A 10 3

WEST (you)   EAST

(a) K 9 4 2   ?
(b) Q J 5
(c) Q 8
(d) K Q J 2

SOUTH

Leads six

(3)   Again declarer is trying to establish a suit at notrump.
This time declarer leads the jack. Do you cover?

DUMMY

♠ A 10 9 8

WEST (you)   EAST

(a) K 4 3   ?
(b) K 4
(c) Q 4 3
(d) Q 4

SOUTH

Leads jack

(4)   It is notrump again, and declarer leads the queen.
Do you cover?

DUMMY

♠ A J 10 8

WEST (you)   EAST

(a) K 4 3   ?
(b) K 9
(c) K 9 4
(d) K 7

SOUTH

Leads queen

(5)   Declarer leads the queen at notrump. Do you cover?

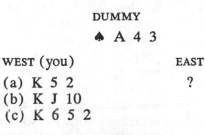

DUMMY

♠ A 4 3

WEST (you)   EAST

(a) K 5 2   ?
(b) K J 10
(c) K 6 5 2

SOUTH

Leads queen

(6)   This time spades are trump and declarer is known to have either a four- or five-card suit. Declarer leads the jack towards dummy. Do you cover?

DUMMY

♠ A 4 3 2

WEST (you)   EAST

(a) Q 5   ?
(b) Q 7 5
(c) K 7 5

SOUTH

Leads jack

Solutions

Part II

(1a)	The seven	When dummy has a broken holding, second hand should play low in order to put declarer to a guess.
(1b)	The five	Same reason as (1a).
(1c)	The two	Same reason as (1a).
(2a)	The two	Do not force honors out of the dummy

		unless you are sure to make a trick for yourself by doing so.
(2b)	The jack	In this case you are making a trick for yourself by playing the jack. Your queen will definitely be a third-round trick. If you play low, declarer might finesse the ten and you will not make any tricks in the suit. (But if dummy holds A K 10 originally, you should play low as you would not be assuring a trick for yourself by playing the jack. Declarer would simply win your jack, return to his hand, and finesse the ten.)
(2c)	The eight	No sense in wasting the queen here. Declarer may well be intending to play the ace and finesse into your queen. Remember that declarer cannot see that you have a doubleton.
(2d)	The jack	Here you should see that by playing one of your equals (always the lower or lowest) you must make two tricks.
(3a)	No	When dummy has *all* the intermediate spot-cards it is impossible to promote anything for your partner. If you can't promote anything for yourself, don't cover.
(3b)	No	Same reason as (3a).
(3c)	No	Same reason as (3a).
(3d)	No	Same reason as (3a).
(4a)	Yes	In case your partner has four cards headed by the nine.
(4b)	No	This time you can't promote anything for yourself or partner.
(4c)	No	Same reason as (4b). Your nine is going to fall the third time the suit is played, so there is no point in covering. The eight is a very big card in dummy.
(4d)	Yes	Same reason as (4a).
(5a)	No	A good declarer will not lead the queen without the jack. Play low, and cover if the jack is led next.
(5b)	Yes	This time you should see that you are go-

ing to promote the jack and ten by covering. Declarer is obviously a beginner to be leading the queen without the jack to back it up. He should be leading *towards* his queen.

(5c) No   This time there are two reasons for not covering: (1) Declarer must have the jack, so you should wait; (2) You have four cards and dummy has only three. It would even be correct to duck twice. The ace will be played the third time and your king will stand up for a sure fourth-round trick. This could easily be the situation:

DUMMY

♠ A 4 3

WEST (you)   EAST

♠ K 6 5 2   ♠ 8 7

SOUTH

♠ Q J 10 9

Notice that if you cover either the queen or the jack with your king, declarer takes four tricks. However, if you duck twice, declarer takes only three.

(6a) No   Declarer must have the ten, so there is no point in covering. Declarer probably has something like K J 10 9 x and may be intending to play the ace and finesse into your queen.

(6b) No   Same reason.

(6c) No   If declarer has the queen you have lost nothing by playing low. For all you know, partner has the queen and it may be a singleton. If you cover, and the ace takes your king and partner's queen at the same time, you had better be a fast talker.

Now for some practical applications. This time you will be shown the entire dummy.

Part III

(a)

               NORTH
               ♠ Q J 10 9
               ♡ K J 9 3
               ◇ A K Q
               ♣ 3 2

WEST (you)   EAST
♠ K 3   ?
♡ A 6 4 2
◇ 7 5 4 3
♣ Q J 10

               SOUTH
                ?

South plays in a contract of 6 ♠, and you decide to lead the queen of clubs. Partner plays the four and declarer wins the ace. At trick two declarer leads a low heart. What do you play and why?

(b)

               NORTH
               ♠ A Q J 9
               ♡ K J 9 3
               ◇ A K Q
               ♣ 3 2

WEST (you)   EAST
♠ K 3   ?
♡ A 6 4 2
◇ 7 5 4 3
♣ Q J 10

               SOUTH
                ?

Once again, you are defending a contract of six spades and you lead the queen of clubs. Partner gives you the same four, and declarer wins the ace.

At trick two declarer leads a low heart. What do you play and why?

(c)   NORTH

♠ A Q J 9
♥ K J 9 3
♦ A K Q
♣ 3 2

WEST (you)   EAST

♠ 8 7   ?
♥ A 6 4 2
♦ 7 5 4 3
♣ Q J 10

SOUTH

?

For the third and final time South plays 6 ♠ and you lead your trusty queen of clubs. Partner plays the nine and declarer wins the ace. At trick two declarer leads a low heart. What do you play and why?

Solutions

Part III

(a)   You should hop up with your ace, because you can see that you will make a trick with your king of spades (you are in back of the ace). In effect, your ace of hearts is the setting trick. It is true that with your possible trump trick (remember you didn't know where the ace of spades was before you made your opening lead) you might have led the ace of hearts. However, the club lead was purposely forced upon you for two reasons. First, to see if you would realize that your ace of hearts was the setting trick upon seeing the dummy; and second, to teach you to watch your partner's signals at trick one. In this case, partner's four of clubs denied possession of the king. Otherwise, he would have signaled with a higher club.

(b)   This time you should play low rather than your ace and hope declarer has two hearts and will finesse dummy's jack. You can see that your king of spades is not going to take a trick, because it is under the ace and the finesse will work for declarer. Your best hope is that partner has the queen of hearts as he obviously does not hold the king of clubs judging from his failure to make an equal honor signal at trick one.

(c)   This time you should hop up with your ace of hearts and immediately play a club. Partner's signal with the nine of clubs has indicated the king. Your ace of hearts and partner's king of clubs are enough to defeat the slam.

KEY POINTERS

(1)   You have just studied one of the most difficult of all aspects of defense play—second-hand play. It is a phase of the game where even experts often come to grief.

(2)   A few of the factors that will assist you in proper second-hand play are:

    (a)   The location of the dummy (to your right or to your left).

    (b)   Whether declarer (or dummy) leads a small card or an honor card.

    (c)   The bidding.

    (d)   Whether the play being made is in the trump suit or a side suit.

    (e)   The number of tricks needed in the suit to defeat the contract.

(3) The general rules to follow so that you don't hold up the game or give away too much information by hesitating are:

(a) *When dummy is to your right:*

1. Cover an honor with an honor unless you see equal honors, in which case you should cover the *last* equal honor.
2. Play low if dummy leads a low card unless you can take the setting trick.
3. If you have three or more equal honors; eg., Q J 10, you should normally play your *lowest* equal.
4. With two equal honors, Q J 7 4, you normally play low. However, if you feel that you should play one of your equals you should play your *lower* equal. (There will be situations later in a hand in which you might want to play one of your equals even though you have only two.)

(b) *When dummy is to your left:*

1. Whenever declarer leads up to a broken holding in dummy K J x, Q 10 x, K 10 x x, second hand should play low, even though he can take the trick. Playing low will give declarer a chance to make an unfortunate guess. (His partner will call it a blunder.)
2. Do not force honors out of the dummy. If the dummy has higher cards than you have, simply *play low*. For example:

DUMMY

♠ A Q 9

WEST (you)

♠ K J 4 2

If declarer leads a spade up to dummy you should
play low. It will do you no good to force one of
dummy's honors by wasting one of your own.
Declarer is going to have to play an honor from
dummy anyway and may even play the ace.
3. If declarer leads either the queen or the jack
   towards a higher honor in the dummy, do not
   cover unless the honor beneath the one declarer
   is leading is visible. In that case, cover only if
   there is a chance for promotion.

DUMMY

♠ A 5 3

WEST (you)   EAST
♠ K 7 5   ?

SOUTH
?

If declarer leads either the queen or the jack,
you should not cover because the honor immediately beneath the honor that declarer has led
is not visible.

DUMMY

♠ A J 3

WEST   EAST
♠ K 6 4   ?

SOUTH
?

Declarer leads the queen, and the honor directly
beneath it is visible. You should cover because
there is a chance for promotion. Partner might
have the ten.

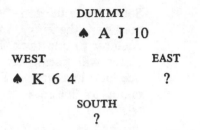

DUMMY

♠ A J 10

WEST   EAST

♠ K 6 4   ?

SOUTH

?

Declarer leads the queen, and the honor directly beneath the honor that declarer is leading is visible. However, there is no chance for promotion, so you should not cover.

4. In this chapter, to avoid confusion, no attention was given to the lead of the ten by the declarer. If declarer leads the ten, second hand must look to see if the jack is visible. If it is not, do not cover; if it is, cover only if there is a chance for promotion.

DUMMY

♠ A 4 3

WEST   EAST

♠ Q 7 6 2   ?

SOUTH

?

South leads the ten. West should not cover because the jack is not visible.

DUMMY

♠ A J 5

WEST   EAST

♠ Q 9 8   ?

SOUTH

?

South leads the ten. West should cover. Partner may have the king, in which case covering holds declarer to one trick. If West plays low, the declarer will finesse the ten and remain with the ace-jack in dummy. This in turn will allow declarer to finesse a second time and make two tricks.

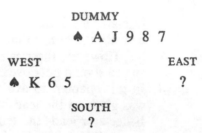

DUMMY

♠ A J 9 8 7

WEST   EAST

♠ K 6 5   ?

SOUTH

?

South leads the ten. The jack is visible, but West should not cover because there is no chance for promotion.

(4) It is helpful if the defenders ask themselves a few key questions as they are confronted with each hand:
 (a) How many tricks do I need to defeat this contract?
 (b) How many can I see in my own hand?
 (c) What has the bidding told me regarding the length of declarer's trump suit, or any suit for that matter?
(5) Keep in mind that to put into practice what you have read in this chapter takes the average player from five to ten years—but that's because he has had no one to teach him how to think.

In any event, don't torture yourself with each play. In case you've forgotten, you are playing bridge to enjoy yourself. Perhaps this chapter wasn't excessively difficult for you. If it was, come back to it every month or so. It is bound to clear up and become a little more meaningful each time.

FURTHER TIPS ON DEFENSIVE PLAY

♠ ♡ ◇ ♣

Now that you've come this far, undoubtedly you have been bitten by the bridge bug and want to improve your game even more.

As was mentioned earlier, in order to be a good defensive player you must:

REMEMBER THE BIDDING

From this you can piece together declarer's distribution and high-card strength.

REMEMBER PARTNER'S OPENING LEAD

From this one card you can often get a count on the suit and have an idea of the location of the missing honor cards.

SELECT THE PROPER CARD WHEN LEADING OR SIGNALING

You must realize that the cards you are playing are influencing your partner's defense; therefore, you should try to lead and signal honestly, not carelessly.

REALIZE THE IMPORTANCE OF PLAYING
THE PROPER EQUAL HONOR

The beginner often thinks that because the Q J 10 are all the same value it doesn't matter which one is played. *Wrong!* In leading from equals, the higher one is played; at all other times, including taking tricks, the lower is used. *At this point we can proceed to two advanced stratagems of defensive play.*

I. USING THE OPPONENT'S BIDDING
TO YOUR ADVANTAGE

You are to assume that you are West, with the following bidding. What assumptions can you make?

SOUTH	WEST	NORTH	EAST
1 ♠	Pass	1 NT	Pass
2 ♠	Pass	Pass	Pass

The questions to ask yourself are:
(1)   How strong is declarer's hand?
(2)   What do I know about his distribution?

If the opening bidder becomes the declarer, you should know from his bidding whether he has a minimum opening bid (13-16 points), an intermediate strength opening (16-18 points), or a powerful opening bid (19-21 points). Bear in mind that the opener's rebid will show his point count if his opening bid has not already done so. He must also clarify his distribution so that his partner can select the proper trump suit. As the opponents relay all this information, the defenders must tune in or they will be lost on defense. In the example sequence, South is showing a minimum opening bid and presumably a six-card spade suit. You might wonder why South can't have a five-card spade suit. Of course he could; but when one receives a one notrump response, which is a weak response that also denies support for opener's major, opener should not *rebid* a

five-card major suit. Therefore, you assume that opener has a
six-card suit with a minimum hand.

Try this one:

SOUTH	WEST	NORTH	EAST
1 ♣	Pass	1 ♡	Pass
2 NT	Pass	3 NT	Pass
Pass	Pass		

We should figure South for about 18-19 points in view of
his *jump* to 2 NT, which is a very common jump rebid. It also
shows a balanced distribution. In other words, opener is unlikely
to have any singletons or voids.

II. COUNTING DECLARER'S TRICKS

When that dummy comes down and you see your partner's
lead, you should attempt to count declarer's tricks. Remember,
when you are playing a hand, especially at notrump, you count
your tricks. Sometimes, although not always, a defender can
also count declarer's tricks. For example:

NORTH (dummy)
♠ 3 2
♡ 7 5
◇ A Q J 10 8 7
♣ A Q 2

EAST
♠ A 7 6 5
♡ Q J 10 9
◇ 4 3 2
♣ 4 3

The bidding:

SOUTH	WEST	NORTH	EAST
1 ♣	Pass	1 ◇	Pass
1 NT	Pass	3 NT	Pass
Pass	Pass		

West leads the queen of spades.

If you are East, this is what you should be thinking. On the bidding, declarer has shown a balanced minimum hand of 13-15 points. Adding your points to dummy's you get twenty; along with declarer's thirteen, this makes a total of thirty-three. In other words, West has a maximum of seven high-card points. (There are 40 high-card points in the deck.)

Now to count declarer's tricks. From the lead, it is apparent that declarer has the king of spades, so that's one trick. There is an imposing diamond suit staring you in the face; and either declarer has the king or partner's king can be finessed, so declarer must be credited with six diamond tricks. In clubs, if declarer has the king he must make at least three tricks; and if partner has the king, it can be finessed. In any case, declarer has two clubs, six diamonds, and one spade. What does this all mean? It means that if you woodenly win the ace of spades and return a spade, declarer will take at least nine tricks. You know that for a certainty because you have just counted declarer's tricks! Your only chance to defeat this contract is to win the ace of spades and return a heart, not a spade.

Your play is justly rewarded because this was the entire deal:

NORTH
♠ 3 2
♡ 7 5
◊ A Q J 10 8 7
♣ A Q 2

WEST
♠ Q J 10 9
♡ A 8 6 4
◊ 5
♣ 10 9 8 7

EAST
♠ A 7 6 5
♡ Q J 10 9
◊ 4 3 2
♣ 4 3

SOUTH
♠ K 8 4
♡ K 3 2
◊ K 9 6
♣ K J 6 5

Had you ducked the first spade or won the ace and returned a spade, declarer would have rattled off the fastest eleven tricks you ever did see. However, with the heart shift the defense can take four heart tricks plus the ace of spades to defeat the contract one trick.

Counting declarer's tricks is not always easy. You must be able to see relationships between your hand and the dummy.

Consider this common situation:

NORTH (dummy)

K 10 9

WEST   EAST (you)

A Q J

SOUTH

You are sitting in back of the king with the ace-queen-jack. You should be able to see that declarer will be unable to get a single trick out of this suit . . . unless you let him.

Assume that declarer leads a low card and finesses dummy's ten. You win with the jack. At this point, the average beginning player would play the ace "to take the trick" but would thus make dummy's king good.

A defender must be very careful about taking tricks if by so doing he is setting up a trick in dummy that would not have been good otherwise. If you win the ten with the jack (defenders take tricks with their lower equals) and play another suit, the next time the suit is led by either declarer or partner you will be in a position to capture dummy's nine with the queen and the king with the ace. Declarer will take no tricks in the suit.

This concept of exiting with another suit rather than taking a trick and thereby setting up a trick or more in dummy is vital to good defense.

Study this layout:

NORTH (dummy)

Q J 9

WEST   EAST (you)

8 7 6 5   A K 10

SOUTH

♠ 4 3 2

Assume that this is a side suit in a trump contract, and West, your partner, leads the eight. Dummy plays the jack, which you win with the king (lower equal). At this point this is what you see in dummy:

DUMMY

♠ Q 9

EAST (you)

A 10

You must realize that if you now take the ace, dummy will play the nine and the queen will be good. But, if you play a different suit and wait for either your partner or declarer to play the suit again, you will be able to capture the queen with the ace and your ten will be high.

As vital as it is not to set up tricks in dummy that would have been unavailable to declarer had you shown more patience, so is it necessary not to be afraid to set up tricks for yourself even if dummy has the high card:

DUMMY

A J 9

WEST   EAST

8 7 6 5   K Q 10

SOUTH

4 3 2

Let's assume that West leads the eight and dummy plays the nine, which East wins with the ten. At this point East should return the king to drive out the ace and make his queen good. *Don't let an ace in dummy frighten you if you have the lower intermediates. Bridge is basically a game of building tricks not just taking them.*

Contrast the above position with this slightly different one:

DUMMY

A J 10

WEST   EAST

8 7 6 5   K Q 9

SOUTH

4 3 2

Again, West leads the eight and dummy plays the ten.

You take the trick with the queen (lower equal when taking tricks) and this is what you see:

DUMMY

A J

WEST   EAST (you)

K 9

SOUTH

This time you cannot afford to return the suit because you will be giving declarer an extra trick in the form of the jack. Again, you must demonstrate your patience by leading a different suit and waiting for either declarer or partner to lead the suit, in which case you will play after dummy and will be able to capture dummy's jack with your king.

Going further, if you see

DUMMY

♠ A K J 10

WEST   EAST (you)

?   ♠ 5 4 2

SOUTH

?

you should assume that declarer can take four tricks in this suit. Either declarer has the queen, in which case four tricks will be easy to take, or partner has it. If partner has the queen he can easily be finessed, so declarer should wind up with four tricks regardless.

Now consider the same dummy but you, East, hold the Q 3 2 of spades. In this case you should count only three tricks for declarer because you must make one trick with your queen *in back of the ace and king.*

Now try this one:

DUMMY

♠ K Q J 9

WEST   EAST (you)

?   (a) A 10 4 3
                     (b) A 8 5 4 3 2
                     (c) 10 6

SOUTH

?

In each case, how many tricks would you figure declarer for in this suit?

(a) You should figure declarer for two tricks. You will take the king with the ace, and after the queen and jack are played your ten will be high. Notice that if you lead the ace instead of waiting to capture an honor, declarer will take three tricks in the suit.

(b)   In this case, declarer figures to take three tricks in the suit because either he has the ten, in which case there is no problem, or else partner's ten will fall under one of dummy's honors.

(c)   In this case, declarer has either three or four tricks depending upon who has the ace. If declarer has the ace he has an easy four tricks, and if partner has the ace your ten is going to fall; declarer will be able to take three tricks rather easily.

In closing, allow me to say that you are learning one of the most beautiful games man has ever created. The more you play the more you will see that each hand is different and that the player who knows when to break the rules is usually the winner.

However, until you have mastered all of the fundamentals presented to you in this series, my suggestion to you is not to purposely make any abnormal bids, plays, or leads; find yourself a congenial partner who is more interested in learning than criticizing; and above all be a pleasant partner and opponent which means making all of your bids in the same tone of voice, no beseeching looks across the table, and no teaching after the hand is over. The player who has made the mistake feels bad enough without being reminded.

Good luck!

Index

INDEX

The Magic of Getting What You Want

Here is the book that could well become your blueprint for personal fulfillment. It was written by one of the foremost authorities on motivation, the author of that enormously successful book *The Magic of Thinking Success*, which has sold more than one million copies.

Now, in this immensely readable, practical, and comforting volume, Dr. Schwartz tells us how we can have more wealth, influence, and happiness by approaching life positively and planning our goals creatively. Dr. Schwartz emphasizes that, after analyzing our special assets and capabilities and deciding what we should do with them, we must also be willing to make certain personal adjustments to get what we want.

Although most of us know what we should be doing with our lives, we need to be reminded of the many ways in which others have achieved their goals. This down-to-earth book is a veritable treasury of inspiration and practical suggestions for everyone who wants to develop a winning philosophy—and, as Dr. Schwartz believes, "a winning philosophy always produces winners."

Find out how to

- Turn your dreams into attainable goals
- Make your mental vision work for you
- Feel confident in any business or social situation
- Win others to your way of thinking

The way you lived yesterday determined your today. But the way you live today will determine your tomorrow. Every day is a new opportunity to become the way you want to be and to have your life become what you want it to be.

Take the first step toward becoming all you're capable of being. Read *The Magic of Getting What You Want* and follow the proven step-by-step plan that can help anyone develop the ultimate in personal power. Then get ready for an incredible adventure that will change you and your life forever.

I invite you to meet an extraordinary princess and accompany her on an enlightening journey. You will laugh with her and cry with her, learn with her and grow with her . . . and she will become a dear friend you will never forget.

Marcia Grad Powers

1 MILLION COPIES SOLD WORLDWIDE

The Princess Who Believed in Fairy Tales

"Here is a very special book that will guide you lovingly into a new way of thinking about yourself and your life so that the future will be filled with hope and love and song."

Og Mandino
Author, *The Greatest Salesman in the World*

The Princess Who Believed in Fairy Tales by Marcia Grad is a personal growth book of the rarest kind. It's a delightful, humor-filled story you will experience so deeply that it can literally change your feelings about yourself, your relationships, and your life.

The princess's journey of self-discovery on the Path of Truth is an eye-opening, inspiring, empowering psychological and spiritual journey that symbolizes the one we all take through life as we separate illusion from reality, come to terms with our childhood dreams and pain, and discover who we really are and how life works.

If you have struggled with childhood pain, with feelings of not being good enough, with the loss of your dreams, or if you have been disappointed in your relationships, this book will prove to you that happy endings—and new beginnings—are always possible. Or, if you simply wish to get closer to your own truth, the princess will guide you.

The universal appeal of this book has resulted in its translation into numerous languages.

Excerpts from Readers' Heartfelt Letters

"*The Princess* is truly a gem! Though I've read a zillion self-help and spiritual books, I got more out of this one than from any other one I've ever read. It is just too illuminating and full of wisdom to ever be able to thank you enough. The friends and family I've given copies to have raved about it."

"*The Princess* is powerful, insightful, and beautifully written. I am seventy years old and have seldom encountered greater wisdom. I've been waiting to read this book my entire life. You are a psychologist, a guru, a saint, and an angel all wrapped up into one. I thank you with all my heart."

Available wherever books are sold or send $15.00 (CA res. $16.24) plus $3.00 S/H to Wilshire Book Co., 9731 Variel Avenue, Chatsworth, California 91311-4315

For our complete catalog, visit our Web site at www.mpowers.com.

The Dragon Slayer
With a Heavy Heart

*This new book by bestselling author Marcia Powers promises to be
one of the most important you will ever read—and one of the most
entertaining, uplifting, and memorable.*

*It brings the Serenity Prayer—which for years has been the guiding
light of 12-step programs worldwide—to everyone . . . and teaches
both new and longtime devotees how to apply it most effectively to
their lives.*

Sometimes things happen we wish hadn't. Sometimes things *don't*
happen we wish *would*. In the course of living, problems arise, both
big and small. We might wish our past had been different or that *we*
could be different. We struggle through disappointments and
frustrations, losses and other painful experiences.

As hard as we may try to be strong, to have a good attitude, not to
let things get us down, we don't always succeed. We get upset. We
worry. We feel stressed. We get depressed. We get angry. We do the
best we can and wait for things to *get* better so we can *feel* better. In
the meantime, our hearts may grow heavy . . . perhaps very heavy.

That's what happened to Duke the Dragon Slayer. In fact, *his*
heart grew *so* heavy with all that was wrong, with all that was not the
way it should be, with all that was unfair, that he became desperate to
lighten it—and set forth on the Path of Serenity to find out how.

Accompany Duke on this life-changing adventure. His guides will
be your guides. His answers will be your answers. His tools will be
your tools. His success will be your success. And by the time he is
heading home, both Duke and you will know how to take life's inevitable lumps and bumps in stride—and find happiness and serenity
anytime . . . even when you really, REALLY wish some things were
different.

"A BEAUTIFUL, EXCEPTIONALLY WELL-WRITTEN STORY THAT CAN HELP
EVERYONE TO BECOME EMOTIONALLY STRONGER AND BETTER ABLE TO
COPE WITH ADVERSITY."   Albert Ellis, Ph.D.
President, Albert Ellis Institute
Author of *A Guide to Rational Living*